THE WORLD IN THE SHADOW OF GOD

THE WORLD IN THE SHADOW OF GOD

An Introduction to Christian Natural Theology

Ephraim Radner

CASCADE *Books* • Eugene, Oregon

THE WORLD IN THE SHADOW OF GOD
An Introduction to Christian Natural Theology

Copyright © 2010 Ephraim Radner. All rights reserved. Except for brief quotations in critical publications or reviews, no part of this book may be reproduced in any manner without prior written permission from the publisher. Write: Permissions, Wipf and Stock Publishers, 199 W. 8th Ave., Suite 3, Eugene, OR 97401.

Revised Standard Version of the Bible, copyright 1952 (2nd edition, 1971) by the Division of Christian Education of the National Council of the Churches of Christ in the United States of America. Used by permission. All rights reserved.

Cascade Books
An Imprint of Wipf and Stock Publishers
199 W. 8th Ave., Suite 3
Eugene, OR 97401

www.wipfandstock.com

ISBN 13: 978-1-60899-017-7

Cataloging-in-Publication data:

Radner, Ephraim, 1956–

The world in the shadow of God : an introduction to Christian natural theology / Ephraim Radner.

viii + 170 p. ; 23 cm. —Includes bibliographical references.

ISBN 13: 978-1-60899-017-7

1. Poetry—21st century—Collections. 2. Natural Theology. 3. Apostles' Creed. I. Title.

PR6063 .I29 R33 2010

Manufactured in the U.S.A.

To Annette:
ad formicam, usque ad caritatem

Contents

Introducing an Introduction to Christian Natural Theology · 1
The Apostles' Creed · 33

1. I · 34
2. Believe · 36
3. In · 37
4. God · 39
5. The Father · 44
6. Almighty · 48
7. Creator · 52
8. Of Heaven · 58
9. And Earth · 59
10. I Believe In · 63
11. Jesus Christ · 65
12. His · 68
13. Only Son · 70
14. Our Lord · 72
15. He Was Conceived · 74
16. By · 75
17. The Power · 77
18. Of the Holy Spirit · 78
19. Born · 79
20. Of the Virgin Mary · 80
21. Suffered · 82
22. Under · 83
23. Pontius Pilate · 87
24. Was Crucified · 90

25 Died · 94
26 And Was · 95
27 Buried · 97
28 He Descended · 100
29 To the Dead · 101
30 On · 102
31 The Third Day · 104
32 He Rose · 106
33 Again · 107
34 He Ascended · 108
35 Into Heaven · 109
36 And Is Seated · 111
37 At · 112
38 The Right Hand of the Father · 113
39 He Will Come Again · 115
40 To Judge · 117
41 The Living · 122
42 And the Dead · 123
43 I Believe In · 124
44 The Holy Spirit · 125
45 The Holy · 130
46 Catholic · 132
47 Church · 136
48 The Communion · 141
49 Of Saints · 146
50 The Forgiveness · 148
51 Of Sins · 149
52 The Resurrection · 152
53 Of the Body · 154
54 And · 155
55 The Life · 156
56 Everlasting · 158
57 Amen · 162

Bibliography · 167

Introducing an Introduction to Christian Natural Theology

This volume attempts two tasks, each one difficult in our own day. First, it ventures into the realm of natural theology, providing in brief span a view of how the world displays the life of God. Second, this first task is pursued, not discursively, but through a range of poems ordered according to the Apostles' Creed. While each task, on its own terms, is hardly a popular exercise in today's Christian culture, taken together, they strain habitual expectation. The following discussion seeks to explain this challenge in its historical context. In the end, I believe there is a strong argument to be made that poetry is a necessary aspect of the Christian faith, in large part because the created world itself is the positive instrument of the Christian faith's practice. The two—poetry and world—go together, and Christian faith itself cannot do, indeed does not exist, without them.

The Nobel Prize-winning physicist and militant atheist Steven Weinberg has expressed a certain regret that the demise of Christian religious belief deprives us perhaps of a significant source of literary inspiration, once evident and forceful in the past at any rate. Where Christian faith has helped positively shape good poetry today, he argues, it is generally in the force of its rejection by the author (e.g., someone like Philip Larkin). But the "wonder" that Weinberg still believes it is possible and good to feel in the face of the natural world, as well as the fear at the annihilation of a bare death that is, in fact, all we have to look forward to, with whatever "good humor" we can muster, is not the last word on faith's cultural dissolution in the West especially. Indeed, it represents itself one aspect that a robust Christian natural theology must itself embrace, as a reflection upon and within the world around us actually discloses the Lord from whom and with whom and towards whom we live, even in the drift of that current that has caught up the "honorable" facing into nothingness that apologists for unbelief like Weinberg have assumed. For even what is nothing takes its shadowed form from something beyond its seeming or perhaps all-too-real emptiness.[1]

It is important that the Christian faith itself struggle with the character of this transitory emptiness, and allow it to speak into the assertions of religious confession and thereby mark out more clearly that confession's contours. This is what a robust natural theology can do, and it is what poetry most especially is bound up in doing.

THE HISTORICAL SHAPE OF NATURAL THEOLOGY

God is apprehended within the world around us, in which we live. But how can this be so? On this question hangs much of our contemporary culture's religious unease.

Taken in its modern sense, "natural theology" is the study of God based on truths that do not derive directly either from Scriptural revelation or authoritative (and inspired) ecclesial discernment. These "natural" truths can include a range of realities, from the physical world to the world of human artifacts and individual or cultural experience. "Natural," in other words, need not refer to non-human or pre-social reality as opposed to human community. But in encompassing the latter, the natural does so without direct reference to or derivation from the Creator towards whom the creature stands, as across an infinite qualitative divide.

And taken in this modern sense, the category of "natural theology" has been a problematic one. But it was not always so, in large measure because this modern sense of "natural theology" has not always exhausted the meaning of the phrase.[2] Borrowing perhaps from the first century BCE Roman writer Varro, it was Augustine who enshrined the topic of *theologia naturalis* as a Christian scholarly focus, referring it to the nature of the gods, and, in its true Christian form, to the "divine nature" itself in its true substance. Hence, natural theology did *not* necessarily exclude, from the start, the presupposition of the Christian God. Rather, its orientation as "natural" marked it as having to do with just such presuppositional categories of even thinking or conceptualizing the Christian

---

1. Weinberg, "Without God," 73–76.
2. The classic survey of Western attitudes through the eighteenth century, including necessarily religious and Christian attitudes, towards "nature" is Clarence J. Glacken's *Traces on the Rhodian Shore*.

God, expecially in relation to other sub- or anti-Christian beliefs. Natural theology, that is, was primarily *metaphysical* in interest, rather than exegetical or doctrinal in the first instance. But if metaphysics might be involved, it would be a metaphysics grounded in, rather than opposed to, divine revelation as a clear coordinate for understanding the "nature" of what is real, with God as the defining center. So Augustine in *The City of God* engages *theologia naturalis* with a free-wheeling investigation into God's standing toward other divine *beings*, and their relation to the world and to causation, including even angels in his discussion.[3]

Natural theology, once pursued in this way, was bound to be unclear in its extent and its boundaries. The Stoic near-identification of "nature" with the divine itself, and the equation of Reason or Logos with the active element of the world as God, provided conceptual handles for some later Christian philosophical metaphysics. Some of these identifications and associations simply crept into the late antique and early medieval discussions and cataloguing of observation and began to offer a storehouse of imagery by which the natural world began to be understood in Christian terms, whatever the blurring of distinctions this might have implied. And so we see works like Isidore of Seville's seventh-century *De Natura Rerum* already opening the way for a metaphysical linkage between matter and God, at least as a means of understanding the world on its own terms as bound to some kind of Christian worldview.

Over the course of the next centuries, we can find among the philosophers and theologians a variety of ways in which an increased overlapping of categories between the realm of material metaphysics and scriptural description leads to the enveloping notions of a "world soul" and a *Natura* that describes this in a way that—again using Stoic terminology of the antique world—draws in the person of God as Spirit.[4] By now, Plato's *Timaeus* has taken on a central role in this conceptualization, as in Bernardus Silvestris's *Cosmographia* from the mid-twelfth century.[5] The

3. See especially Books 8 through 11.

4. For an essay on aspects of this period, rich with primary- and secondary-source references, see Mews, "World As Text," 95–122. One aspect that is not discussed here and that deserves more study is the relationship of Jewish notions of creation as bound to Torah to developing Christian conceptions of Nature's "book."

5. See the fine introduction by Winthrop Witherbee to his translation of the *Cosmographia*, in Witherbee, *Cosmographia of Bernardus Silvestris*, 1–62. C. S. Lewis's *The Discarded Image* still provides a wonderfully vivid and accessible entry into the

historical place of movements like Franciscan "inductive" spirituality (cf. Bonaventure's Platonically informed *The Mind's Journey into God*), that sought to move the contemplative mind from a consideration of God's creatures to their Creator, seems to be related, if unclearly, to these developments. The "books" of Nature and of Scripture had by now, in any case, been seen to rest concordant (if not synonymous) one with another, a conviction well established into the seventeenth century, as Drummond's famous sonnet lays out, "Of this fair volume which we World do name. . . ."

The blurring of philosophical and theological categories over this period, however, should not be seen in itself as a corruption of Christian realism. For even in its appropriation of non-Christian conceptions, the purpose of these discussions was always to elucidate something that Scripture itself was seen as centrally affirming: "ever since the creation of the world [God's] invisible nature, namely, his eternal power and deity, has been clearly perceived in the things that have been made," in Paul's words (Rom 1:20). How can the world *not* witness to, even "reveal" God? And more so, how might we deny this in a specifically *Christian* sense, when the Apostle also tells us that "in him [Christ, the Son] all things were created, in heaven and on earth, visible and invisible, whether thrones or dominions or principalities or authorities—all things were created through him and for him" (Col 1:16). If nothing else, the "visible world" of "secondary causes," as Gregory of Nazianzus eloquently urged, was so marvelously fraught with mystery that at the least it unveiled the *greater* veil of God's marvelous being, which only the revelation of Christ could indicate directly.[6] In general, then, "natural theology" necessarily remained bound, for all its occasional odd stirrings and departures, to a scriptural ontology, much as Augustine himself seemed to presuppose.

A more noticeable decoupling between nature and Scripture, theologically speaking, begins in the sixteenth century and achieves completion in the seventeenth, at least according to compelling scholarly arguments such as those by Michael Buckley. Much of the impetus for this comes from a new questioning of religious tradition itself, including the Scriptures, growing out of an array of building forces from Renaissance

---

"Model" universe of many medieval thinkers, with all of the "foregrounding" descriptive interest this provided, upheld as it was by the confidence of a divinely wrought world.

6. Gregory of Nazianzus, "Second Theological Oration," esp. chapters 30–31.

and Reformation habits and dislocations. With a developing science of the observable world moving forward, both in terms of biology and physics, as well as in the documentary sciences of critical history, the "natural" came to have its own integral place *apart from* scriptural metaphysical conceptualities—including revelation—in which it had always previously found its home.

In particular, natural theology became more and more tied to the question of theistic "proof," and the character of human knowledge's foundations. Although the notion and formulation of "proofs of God" were already engaged in the Middle Ages, often on the basis of categories and conceptions derived from Augustinian exemplars (something that continued in the sixteenth and seventeenth centuries), they did not achieve a special status as apologetic disciplines in their own right. But by the seventeenth century it was just such independence of apprehension that began to be clamored after, in the face of growing public disputes over the rational and persuasive bases of conflicting ecclesial and religious claims. Whether moving from deductive premises, or ordering thought from inductively arranged data, the form and nature of God would be presented, so it was thought, in an almost necessary manner.

Summarizing the work of a Christian apologist and scholar like Leonard Lessius (1554–1623), who re-deployed Stoic "topics" in a new battle against Europe's emerging class of religious skeptics, Buckley writes:

> Natural theology, then, becomes no longer a part of metaphysics, but derivative by common sense of ordinary philosophic maxims from astronomy, comparative religion, mechanics, and biology. It is a world to which theology itself has very little contribution to make. So it remains in the centuries to come, an effort to provide a preamble to Christian convictions about god which does not include Christ.[7]

Only a few writers at the time accepted Spinoza's neo-Stoic identification of this realm with God himself—*deus sive natura*[8]—an identification by

---

7. Buckley, *At the Origins of Modern Atheism*, 55.

8. Spinoza, *Ethics*, IV, Preface. That Spinoza in fact derived his phrase from a medieval Jewish tradition, popular in his time, of equating the numerical value of the letters of *elohim* (God, as in the creation accounts of Genesis) and *ha-teba'* (the material world) (86), has been argued by Moshe Idel; see his "*Deus sive Natura*—The Metamorphosis of

which the divine was actually drawn *away* from revelation and church into a more exclusive natural orbit than "theology" formally understood. But even stopping short of such a move, natural theology came to be seen increasingly as an alternative and even rival to Christian scriptural and ecclesial *doctrina*, with its own subject matter, rules, and arguments.

The subversion of *sacra doctrina* was not, by and large, the intention of most Christian natural theologians in the early modern world. From Robert Boyle through John Ray (not to mention the more lugubrious Thomas Burnet), Bernard Nieuwentyt, J. C. Lesser, and finally the most successful (and currently intellectually vilified) exemplar of orthodox natural theology, William Paley, the study of natural phenomena was viewed as a buttress to the Christian faith against rationalistic and even skeptical atheism.[9] It was also viewed, however and in its own right, as a means of devotion and joyful worship of God. And certainly for moral theologians like Joseph Butler (and Paley, in his own way) natural theology provided a wondrous opening by which the shape of the Christian life might be seen as coherent with the general shape of the world (although not without pain for all that).[10]

David Hume, to be sure, attempted to deal a death-blow to these kinds of hopes. In his *Dialogues on Natural Religion*, as well as in his *Natural History of Religion* from the mid-eighteenth century, he sought both to subvert the logic of drawing metaphysical (and religious) conclusions from observed phenomena and to offer an ersatz "historical" explanation for the (perhaps inescapable) rise of religious belief. Kant, for his part, tried to make a virtue of Hume's skepticism in these regards, canonizing the rational limitations of the religious imagination as a kind of human distillate to be gratefully but responsibly used in translated hu-

---

a Dictum from Maimonides to Spinoza," 87–110.

9. For Barth, this all proved to be a failed Christian apologetic in the face of secular rationalism; its arguments were bound to crumble precisely because it had adopted a rationalist framework itself, incapable of dealing with an unruly and fallen world. Cf. Karl Barth, *Protestant Theology in the Nineteenth Century*, 145. Barth alludes here to Lesser's remarkable work. Even Barth, however, cannot hide a certain admiration for this robust "lay" approach to apologetics, although he articulates a distinct negative amusement with its naïve self-delusion.

10. To this extent, Newman was wrong in claiming that "in the Protestant school of Paley and other popular writers, the idea of Natural Theology had practically merged in a scientific view of the argument from Design" (in "On Consulting the Faithful in Matters of Doctrine," 202).

man form. These kinds of arguments had a cumulative effect, especially as the religious imagination, as Kant would conceive it, was itself the object of increasing disdain and suspicion from many quarters of institutionally aggrieved Europeans. It was never clear, in any case, what to *do* with the religious leftovers of these debates, and philosophical theism has never found a social niche beyond dark corners of the academy.

Ultimately, with the elaboration of the natural sciences as well as the establishment of anti-ecclesial rationalism within European educated society, the distinction between the objects of natural theology and scriptural metaphysics grew into an actual rupture. Despite the efforts of natural theologians as wildly disparate as Coleridge and Philip Henry Gosse—both of whom, in their own ways (along with many others in the nineteenth century still) were caught up in the astonishing combustion brought about by the Bible and the Church's encounter with naturalistic description—the rupture proved in fact to be a widening chasm. It was one that perhaps encouraged and certainly was used to promote broad and specific intellectual movements seeking to overthrow altogether the adequacy of traditional theology's claims. In the place of such claims, many "natural theologians" sought to provide newly constructed descriptions of God that could be asserted as coherent with developing scientific understandings of the world, sometimes directly addressing Hume and Kant, sometimes simply plowing ahead as if they had never raised their questions. "Natural theology" came to have for its practitioners a greater stature, in terms of truth, than doctrinally oriented theologies set forth within the Church's seminaries. An established churchman like Charles Raven in the twentieth century could certainly maintain his place within the classical structures of the Church; but his work led him to question in many ways the classic tenets of the Church he served.

Roman Catholics tended to eschew the conflict, by and large. Still, the last century has seen a growing unanimity among traditional Christians, classically enunciated by Karl Barth, that "natural theology" in its modern sense—and perhaps in all senses—is both useless and probably even corrupting of the Church's understanding of God.[11] From Barth's perspective, natural theology fails fundamentally because it cannot, by definition, "observe" the world as it "really is," both in its relationship with God in Christ and in its rebellion against that relationship. Any attempt to describe the

---

11. Barth, "No! Answer to Emil Brunner," 151–67.

world, and from that description to illuminate God, apart from or prior to the truth of God's being in Christ, is *a priori* a deceptive task that gives rise to a deceiving fruit.

Not everyone who has objected to natural theology in our day on these grounds—not even, perhaps Barth himself, ultimately—would necessarily wish to undercut the possibility of knowing God through the world that God has made. But the construal of that world's theologically descriptive capacity has been profoundly altered by the suspicion now almost universally cast upon natural theology's modern argument with *sacra doctrina*. Stanley Hauerwas, while building on Barth's classic articulation of that suspicion, has for instance, sought some kind of descriptively based theological indicator within the phenomenologically rooted "witness" of Christian service in the world. Such witness, he claims, through its very coherence with God's will in Christ, attests to the "way things really are." This *is* a kind of adjustment towards that which he has earlier precluded, as Hauerwas himself admits when he speaks, following Barth, of a "recovery of natural theology as a Christological theme."[12] But it may go further even than he realizes. For if Hauerwas is right, and proper Christian witness provides a rational response to, and language to talk about, God's self-revelation, then it becomes possible to recover the value of much of the human-centered discussion that provided the modernist project that seemed to render purposefully inadequate the world's indication of God: will not the Christian life, in its depth of integrity, finally permit coherence to emerge, however odd such coherence might seem to those whose eyes are still not used to the light?

The issue here has to do with the contours of the perceived world—both its own outlines, as it were (assuming they exist in and of themselves somehow), and the powers of perception belonging to those who apprehend it. Just as pertinently, then, there has been, in the wake of Barth's writing in particular, a desire to grapple with the very character of creation in its intrinsic and intrinsically ordered relationship to God, *just because* of the Christian claim that any truly "natural theology," in its original sense, must be bound up with the metaphysics of God's own self-revealing. In other words, the "rupture" between nature and revelation that seems to have overwhelmed natural theology in the modern era is perhaps itself wrongheaded and in need of reconceiving.

12. Hauerwas, *With the Grain of the Universe*, 159.

Ephraim Radner

ANALOGY AS IMITATION

Natural theology has had its own recent resurgence in some circles of religious philosophy. The apologetic motive, frankly, is still very much at one with the seventeenth century's, although the field has changed dramatically in the combat, with Christian belief clearly requiring (and having expected of it within the academy) a set of less-assertive claims. And so the claims of atheism are now met, not by offering "proof" as much as by saying that such a demand and response is in fact inappropriate and unnecessary. On offer instead are the alternatives of a kind of rational probabilism. These are given in theistic terms or even as aspects of particular Christian beliefs, or of a certain presuppositional logic of individual and communal faith that need not so much rely on "proof" or "evidence" as on a certain coherent reasonableness that has its place within the pluralistic realm of rational human life as a whole. By and large, contemporary natural theologians tend to side-step basic questions of induction and deduction, and so avoid the attacks of a Humean kind or the skepticism of the anti-Kantians. But in so doing, they have still left open the possibility of a weaker kind of "induction," more akin to a devotional practice, whereby the things of this world can contribute and play a part in one's deepening apprehension of God, without however needing to play an essential or foundational role.[13] Even here, though, questions arise and thrust us back to earlier arguments and worries.

One of the more contentious areas of natural theology among *Christian* theologians in the last fifty years has centered on the question of "analogy," and in particular whether there is and how we are to understand any analogy of creation's reality with its Creator, that is, with God. It should be said that the very notion of an analogy of creation is rooted in a Christian (or at least Judeo-Christian) metaphysic. Even to discuss it as a possible way of understanding the nature of the world—or "nature" itself—is, for many, to locate natural theology in a pre-modern framework. Barth's early rejection of such talk of analogy (particularly the form used, he thought, by Roman Catholic theologians), and his continuing reluctance to use it himself in any form, has proven a major point of debate. How can the creature, in its intrinsic rebellion against God, in its infinite

---

13. Basic examples here would be Richard Swinburne's *The Existence of God*; and Alvin Plantinga and Nicholas Wolterstroff's *Faith and Rationality*.

qualitative distance from God, and in its exclusively defined character in relation to the pure graciousness of God in Christ, ever be an indicator, apart from the latter, of God in terms that could be truthful?

But the very notion of an "analogy"—of metaphysical "being" or of form or of reality—between creature and Creator orients the discussion in a way that Barth was perhaps not as sensitive to and even as appreciative of as he ought to have been. Creature and Creator demand, in their very utterance and use as words and concepts, the application of presuppositions, at least, that assert fundamental relationships that are described only on the basis of "revelation." Indeed, the words cannot be deployed even apart from some kind of grammar, even narrative grammar, that must appropriate particular claims, in the Christian case, of Scripture. Why then the worry over their secularly imported status?

And so Thomas Aquinas, who represents a classic (if diversely interpreted) exponent of the notion of analogy in this case, speaks of the relationship in terms given to him by the Scriptures themselves: "wisdom," for instance. And this is the question: how shall we understand the use the Scripture itself makes of a term like "wise" as applied both to creature (for which we have some habitual conception) and Creator, whose "wisdom" must indeed seem incongruous in every way with the word's cultural usage? Whatever similarities exist between human and divine "wisdom," Thomas writes, it cannot be a similarity of identity that is being expressed linguistically: "it should be said that the Creator and the creature are reduced to one, not by community of univocation but by community of analogy." There are different kinds of analogy, Thomas goes on to explain. For instance, some things are "analogous" because they are both aspects, in different ways, of one reality (e.g., act and potency are both aspects of "being" and are thus analogous). But in the case of those aspects of God that we speak of in natural terms, the "analogy" has to do, he says, with the fact that one thing has caused the other: "one thing receives existence and meaning from the other, and such is the analogy of creature to the Creator: the creature does not have existence except to the extent that it has come down from the first being." Thomas calls this kind of analogy "imitation," a similarity between the thing caused and the Cause itself: "Hence the creature is not called a being except insofar as it imitated the first being; and it is the same concerning wisdom and all the other things that are said of the creature."[14]

The notion that there is some resemblance between the thing caused and its cause is, in itself, not entirely clear. But it derives—and even Thomas's language of "descent" does this literally—from scriptural claims, like that of Jas 1:17: "Every good gift and every perfect gift is from above, coming down from the Father of lights." This notion, furthermore, has formed the basis even of developing modern Christian natural theology that, finally, Barth himself came to distrust so deeply. The eighteenth- and nineteenth-century Methodist commentator Adam Clarke provides an effusive catalogue, precisely of natural theology's practitioners and their labors, on the basis of the "descending" analogy. While discussing, on Exodus 28, the fashioning of the priestly vestments for the Tabernacle's service, Clarke follows a traditional exegetical move (dating even from pre-Christian Jewish commentary and taken up by the fathers) on this text by seeing the detailed ornament of the garments as depicting somehow—analogously—the beauteous wonder of creation, now also (analogously) represented through the creative artistry of the human craftsman:

> This principle, that God is the author of all arts and sciences, is too little regarded: Every good gift, and every perfect gift, says St. James, comes from above, from the Father of Lights. Why has God constructed every part of nature with such a profusion of economy and skill, if he intended this skill should never be discovered by man, or that man should not attempt to examine his works in order to find them out? From the works of Creation what proofs, astonishing and overwhelming proofs, both to believers and infidels, have

---

14 Thomas Aquinas, *Commentary On the Sentences of Peter Lombard*, I., Prologue, Q. 1 a.2. The terms are sufficiently precise as to merit citation in the original Latin: "Ad secundum dicendum, quod Creator et creatura reducuntur in unum, non communitate univocationis sed analogiae. Talis autem communitas potest esse duplex [dupliciter]. Aut ex eo quod aliqua participant aliquid unum secundum prius et posterius, sicut potentia et actus rationem entis, et similiter substantia et accidens; aut ex eo quod unum esse et rationem ab altero recipit, et talis est analogia creaturae ad Creatorem: creatura enim non habet esse nisi secundum quod a primo ente descendit: [unde] nec nominatur ens nisi inquantum ens primum imitatur; et similiter est de sapientia et de omnibus aliis quae de creatura dicuntur." Latin text in Thomas Aquinas, *Scriptum Super Libros Sententiarum Magistri Petri Lombardi Episcopi Parisiensis*, 10. Other versions can be found at the Peter Lombard site of the Franciscan Archive. Online: http://www.franciscan-archive.org/lombardus/index.html. The English translation referred to here is by Br. Alexis Bugnolo, edited by Hugh McDonald and available at this site.

been drawn both of the nature, being, attributes, and providence of God! What demonstrations of all these have the Archbishop of Cambray, Dr. Neuwentyt, Dr. Derham, and Mr. Charles Bonnet, given in their philosophical works! And who gave those men this wisdom? God, from whom alone Mind, and all its attributes, proceed. While we see Count de Buffon and Swammerdam examining and tracing out all the curious relations, connections, and laws of the Animal kingdom; Tournefort, Ray, and Linne, those of the Vegetable; Theophrastus, Werner, Klaproth, Cronstedt, Morveau, Reamur, Kirwan, and a host of philosophical chemists, Boerhaave, Boyle, Stahl, Priestley, Lavoisier, Fourcroy, Black, and Davy, those of the Mineral; the discoveries they have made, the latent and important properties of vegetables and minerals which they have developed, the powerful machines which, through their discoveries, have been constructed, by the operations of which the human slave is restored to his own place in society, the brute saved from his destructive toil in our manufactories, and inanimate, unfeeling Nature caused to perform the work of all these better, more expeditiously, and to much more profit; shall we not say that the hand of God is in all this? [. . .] He alone girded those eminent men, though many of them knew him not; he inspired them with wisdom and understanding; by his all- pervading and all-informing spirit he opened to them the entrance of the paths of the depths of science, guided them in their researches, opened to them successively more and more of his astonishing treasures, crowned their persevering industry with his blessing and made them his ministers for good to mankind. The antiquary and the medalist are also his agents; their discernment and penetration come from him alone. By them, how many dark ages of the world have been brought to light; how many names of men and places, how many customs and arts, that were lost, restored! And by their means a few busts, images, stones, bricks, coins, rings, and culinary utensils, the remaining wrecks of long-past numerous centuries have supplied the place of written documents, and cast a profusion of light on the history of man, and the history of providence. And let me add, that the providence which preserved these materials, and raised up men to decipher and explain them, is itself gloriously illustrated by them.

Of all those men (and the noble list might be greatly swelled) we may say the same that Moses said of Bezaleel and Aholiab: "God hath filled them with the Spirit of God, in wisdom, and in understanding, and in knowledge; and in all manner of workmanship, to devise cunning works; to work in gold and in silver, and in brass, in cutting of stones, carving of timber, and in all manner of workmanship;" chap. xxxi. 3–6. "The works of the Lord are great, sought out of all them that have pleasure therein;" Psa. cxi. 2.[15]

The work of imitation is here described in terms of "inspiration," something that perhaps is less obvious in Thomas's more general discussion. But it is an inspiration that works more deeply than simply in the efforts and accomplishments of singularly chosen individuals. For, as eighteenth-century writers like Robert Lowth began to recognize,[16] it is the same Spirit who leads individual poets who also creates each element of the world that the poet praises, and finally is the Author of Scripture's words themselves. (Or, indeed, one could speak—as does Maximus the Confessor—of the creative Word whose "words" not only directly take form in the Scriptures, but found the ability of human beings to speak their own words at all.) Indeed, the analogy is "latent" in creation itself, and its imitative character is itself a part of the inspiring work of God, whose description and articulation are given particular form by artists, but hardly invented by them. Indeed, the artist shares with his work the common Cause that draws them together, so that speech or crafted expression become bound up inextricably with the very nature of their created analogy. What is "imitative" is *this* history of createdness from the one God; and this history necessarily repeats in different ways and according to different aspects the singular and inescapable relation that is God's initiating formation of all things.

---

15. Clarke, *Holy Bible*, 442. Clarke was imbued with his era's Christian vision of God's providential ordering of creation, as evidenced by the lists of authors he cites here. He himself provided a much re-printed translation (1804) of Christophe Christian Sturm's long set of daily devotions on the divine character of the natural world (*Reflections on the Works of God in Nature and Providence*). Clarke's own Methodist theological influence, furthermore, picked these aspects up and passed them along to the nineteenth-century Holiness tradition in a way that belies, to an interesting extent, contemporary criticisms of a purported evangelical denigration of nature.

16. Cf. Lowth, *Lectures on the Sacred Poetry of the Hebrews*, Lectures 1, 16, and 17. Lowth's discussion of "passionate" imitation, bound to God's Spirit, as the basis of all poetry, underlay his conviction regarding "religious" poetry's supreme value as a form of pure "praise."

ANALOGY AS SHADOW

There is clearly a problem, however, with conceiving of natural theology as the articulation of that imitative analogy of creature to Creator that obtains in a broad and exhaustive way with respect to the natural world. In the first place, there is the simple challenge of accurately describing the form of the analogy itself, so as not to distort its divine implications, and thereby its moral conclusions from a human point of view. If human wisdom is analogous to God's own wisdom, as object to its cause, we must nonetheless first be able to describe the shape of human wisdom itself if the claim is to have even a devotional focus of accuracy.

To those (like Hobbes,[17] not to mention even Solomon, as in Prov 6:6) who saw, for instance, among the ants a moral analogy for human life (however imperfect), legitimated if even only implicitly by its divine origin, scientists like Julian Huxley declared that all such analogizing was entirely perverted: "Innumerable comparisons have been made between human society and the social organisation of ant, bee, or termite . . . [and] almost without exception the moral has been false."[18] So the geologist and poet Jonathan Wonham has argued as well: what exactly we find analogous seems to reflect less the First Cause than the simple cultural prejudices of the observer. In Caryl Haskins's 1939 *Of Ants and Men*,[19] Wonham argues by example, Haskins

> compares the evolution of three major ant groups: the Ponerines, the Myrmicines and the Formicines to "evolution" of human society from primitives, to empire-builders and, finally, to pioneers. Of Ponerines he says: "The young are, for ants, extremely athletic, competent, and able to care for themselves, exactly as the children of primitive peoples display an early competence which belies their

---

17. Thomas Hobbes, *Leviathan*, II.17. Hobbes follows Aristotle in calling the ants (and bees) "political" in their organization, and notes, with others, how they manage this without coercive "direction." Humans, however, are unable so to organize themselves without some directive force applied, for a host of causes: their innate competitiveness, their rationality that gives rise to individualism and negative and selfish judgments, their ability to talk that even furthers these dynamics, and so on. The analogy between ants and human being in society is real, but useful especially insofar as it discloses the deep differences between "natural" and "artificial" conditions, that latter ruled, in human terms, by yet deeper natural limitations.

18. Huxley, *Ants*, 1.

19. Haskins, *Of Ants and Men*.

later deficiency." Or: "the ease with which the entire economy of the colony may be overturned by a very slight alteration of the environment all bespeak primitiveness." So much for Ponerines who are, eventually, dismissed as carnivorous, barbaric and always on the move looking for new prey on which to feast. The Myrmicines, with their "Queen found[ing] colonies among inhospitable regions' sound like agents of the British Empire. And the Formicine resemble, more than anything, the doughty American homesteaders of the frontier, 'pushing' hard upon the edges of the (American continent's) melting glaciers . . . an aggressive, sensitive band of pioneer Formicines" whose "simplicity in social life is evident" and who rely on their own resourcefulness.[20]

Who is to say, in retrospect, if Haskins's ants did not indeed unlock, through analogy, the meaning of humankind in 1939?

Still, 1939's organic resemblances are a far cry from God's own hand tilting the world. Those who speak of the ants at best describe themselves, and perhaps that only uniquely and mischievously. If we "go to the ant" (Prov 6:6) and "ask the beasts" (Job 12:7), shall we hear "wisdom" or more likely, the corruption of wisdom? So what shall we say of imitative analogy, other than at best that it is a hope whose gift is rendered vain by the reality of the malleable human heart and perhaps even (as Burnet wondered) the figural vacuity of all living things, such that the "beast" is left only to point out sin, a usage the Desert Fathers eagerly employed?

But in fact, among those most wedded to the scholastic doctrine of analogy are those most aware of its moral limitations. God is "transcendent" to all "transcendents" as we might imagine them, Henri Bouillard writes. Even "being," as in the proposition that "God *is*," cannot be understood as a predicate, so as to introduce into God's reality a category that is simply common to all things, including ourselves. And so the early twentieth-century Thomist Antonin-Dalmace Sertillanges turns to Aquinas's citation from Gregory the Great: *balbutiendo ut possumus excelsa Dei resonamus* ("Even in our stammering, we are able to sound out the marvelous things of God").[21] This is a matter of grace, to be sure, but a grace, grasped negatively if looked at squarely, embedded in the forms of our creaturely existence. Even the term "perfection" is not adequate for

20. Wonham, "The Ant Analogy." Online: www.http://qarrtsiluni.com.
21. Thomas Aquinas, *Summa Theologiae*, 1a, 4.1 ad 1, quoting Gregory the Great in the *Moralia* 5.26, 29.

the Uncreated who alone creates. To use such defining words as "cause," writes Sertillanges, therefore "implies no more than the postulate of universal poverty."[22]

By speaking of "poverty" Sertillanges turns to the general category of creaturely limitation, as though there are outlines that bind the creature's sense and experience, and beyond which its pressing cannot move even though that press itself is somehow driven towards God. Impossibilities hound the very being of the creature. Even Barth saw mortality as a king of natural "historical witness" to God, although hardly of the same kind as Revelation.[23] And hence Sertillanges is talking about more than an experiential limit upon knowledge. He is alluding as well to the moral failure involved in a "poverty" whose reach is exhaustive, so that the "outlines" of a creature and its experience represent also the shape of one's interior perceptions and reactions. Thus, all creatures come into confrontation with their "outlines." But these outlines are also "inlines," in the sense that they define every aspect of creatureliness as also a kind of inevitable withering: for who are we, if we cannot know even who we "really" are? Are we not destined simply to drift away? Do we not "pass as a shadow," therefore, neither knowing our coming nor our going (Eccl 6:12)?

Perhaps this kind of judgment is already too interpretively shaped within a Christian mode of thinking. But that is the nature of Christian natural metaphysics. Indeed, the claim here regarding the analogical character of human experience and apprehension—of the "world" as it is bound to human life somehow—is that it speaks of God, even when and especially and fundamentally only (because this only is what can happen) when somehow one has failed to speak rightly of God at all. This too marks the outline, not of God but of what God has made. Yet having made it, it is His, and will ever be such. We might speak of analogy here in terms of a "shadow" with its ambivalent character of outline from without but also darkness and threat as it somehow obscures some limited and perhaps even false hope from within. Indeed, the scriptural language of "shadow" as pertaining to God is itself somewhat ambiguous: protective

---

22. Bouillard, *Connaissance de Dieu*, 158–59; citation from Sertillanges, *La Philosophie de S. Thomas d'Aquin*, 173–74.

23. There are four such historical indicators, according to Barth: the history of Scripture, Church history, the history of Israel, and human mortality itself. See the *Church Dogmatics* III/3; also Lindsay, *Barth, Israel, and Jesus*, 74–75.

(Ps 17:8; 91:1), overcoming and even deathly (Isa 25:5; Jer 6:4; 13:16), creatively instrumental at a distance (Acts 5:15), looming out in awesome and revelatory glory (Matt 17:5), incomplete (Jonah 4:5-8), even somehow inappropriate (Jas 1:17). But for all that, "heavenly" shadows form the connective tissue of natural history and divine reality (Col 2:17; Heb 8:5; 10:1), and the world exists just in this form, marked by the overcast of goodness and heaven. Much as the Law is "holy, just and good," is in fact "spiritual," yet it drives us to our knees in a recognition of "wretchedness" before God who alone can turn this—yet *just this!*—into "thanksgiving" (Rom 7:12, 14, 24, 25), so our "natural" lives drive us to God as they drive us against our own perplexed inner and outer walls.

Obviously, the sense that God casts a shadow upon the world, indeed, that the world is filled with or even somehow stands towards God as a set of shadows derived from some further and ungrasped substantial form, scriptural though the metaphor is, was prone to a range of more strictly philosophical and Platonic elaborations. But the metaphor remains implanted all the same, and works on at least two levels: precisely by grasping the material aspect of creation and claiming this analogically to its Creator and Cause; yet also by insisting that its character as a "natural" life be imbued with a fundamental ambivalence and ambiguity, so that its turn toward God even proves to be the source of diverse and perhaps distorted claims. In our imitation of God, that is, we are knotted, at least in ourselves, to the moral ambiguities and even abject failures of the shadow's passing.

And leaving aside the redemption of such imitation as itself a form of life—for we are speaking naturalistically here—we must at least root the shadowed analogy of our being there where imitation is most consciously and exclusively embodied, where it is most clearly the motor of meaning: poetry, the artifacted remains, beset by time, of the natural man. That poetry is itself an "imitation" of nature has been a standard claim since antiquity—as indeed, all forms of human artifice follow the "pattern" of what the world, or "nature" has given us ("every art is an imitation of nature," in Seneca's famous dictum[24]), with "nature" here, in its more ancient sense as inclusive of the world as a whole, rather than exclusive. For Plato, this very fact rendered poetry problematic, because as an "imitation" (*mimesis*), it represented an inherently degraded form of something else that

---

24. "Omnis ars naturae imitatio est." Seneca *Moral Epistles* (65.3) 444–45.

is more real than its replica. Indeed, Plato makes negative use of the kind of theological dynamic set up later by Christian assertions of analogy's infinite distance from the transcendent God.[25] In this case, the artist copies the copy (nature) of what is the most real, the Idea, and here the "descent" is a fall into inevitable deformity and error. For Aristotle, who more systematically and influentially formulated the notion of poetry as natural imitation, the problem was less compelling because his own metaphysic found what was "real" within this or that thing or action itself, as it were, rather than seeing things and actions simply as a dilution of something else more real. The "representation of life" that poetry "naturally" strives after is an imitation of the meaning of actual existence in the world, in its fullness. Hence, poetry could usefully—through its mimetic function—disclose the "nature" of existence through its storied depictions of "probable" and "necessary" actions and their consequences. Rather than simply and inevitably engendering base emotions, leading the listener or reader astray from what is real, Aristotle believed that poetry's ability to move a person could properly, if skillfully and responsibly done, lead someone to a knowledge capable of distinguishing good and evil in the world.[26]

However one decides the issue of the relative moral usefulness of imitative poetry, both Plato and Aristotle share the mimetic presupposition that language is inherently descriptive. It is descriptive not simply because of its character as correspondent to the external world, but as bound up with the limits and substances of human existence within that world, that is, as expressive of the brute realities of worldly life because speech is itself an appendage of an organism, it is itself "natural." Hence, language can indeed and necessarily does represent the "good and the bad," however defined; and the "nature" represented here, of course, would include more than physical reality, but also the reality of the mind and spirit, such as that might be. It is a "thing's" reality that makes it describable, even the passions of an unruly heart, and its reality subjects that description to a measure, however debated, of accuracy or truth.

Language itself is "natural," not only in its origin as arising from within human experience, but as representative of that experience sim-

---

25. See Plato's *Republic* III.377–92 and X.595–602 especially.

26. Aristotle's *On the Art of Poetry* ("Poetics") is organized on the principle of *mimesis*, as is well known. His discussion of tragic poetry, in cc. 6–18, contains the meat of his theory.

ply and necessarily. For a Christian, language is thereby rightly seen as *creaturely* in this way as well and thus is a part of and a descriptor of the shadowed character of creaturely existence as a whole. If, for a Christian like Augustine, language as a sign-system is penultimate, it is because of this arrested reach. But even he, in the face of the Incarnation, could not quite rid himself of the intrinsically demanded imitative character of "the world" understood positively, although now with a new ordering in which all is shown to proceed through and to Christ, rather than apart from him. On the one hand, the whole creation—just as all gracious artifacts—speaks out in its own language that "God has made me!"; and it does so in a way that, because of its vastness, even in this limited fashion must escape human language. On the other hand, in Christ the "Head," God *is* truly praised in fullness, through faith and witness (much as Hauerwas would have us believe). There is a necessary speaking by creation of what God has made and hence of God, and there is a necessary failure in that speech; there is an even deeper speaking that is done only in Christ, and entered into through the giving up of words to him as one gives up life itself to him who has first given it and held it.[27] Hence, poetic imitation in a Christian sense—the word that praises rightly—becomes not simply a description of the "way things are," but turns into an imperative, driven by choices, stops and starts, failures and accomplishments, faithfulness and love that is swept along, and from God's own grace reveals him in the redemptive form of his mediation—not disjunctively from the world, but as the center of the world. The Word is given in words—his own, but his own because he has drawn our speech into the creative force of his speaking. What does language imitate, then, if allowed simply to speak, if finally unfettered as the Word unfettered (2 Tim 2:9)? It imitates the Cross and the Resurrection both, the divine sacrifice of humility given in life-creating love in the face of sin and for the sake of sinners.

But even this word, apprehended by the Christian, is hardly a logical word, especially when simply ordered in terms of the world's form. This is the character of the shadow, and it explains why the imitative role of poetry was ever pressed by ethical scruples to clarify its purpose, to

---

27. Cf. Augustine *Expositions of the Psalms* the second discourse on Psalm 27(26). On the character of Jesus as God's "spoken word," that is, a sign that founds the possibility of signs, who is yet a signless Wisdom, see for instance *Christian Doctrine* I.12–14 and *City of God* X.2.

evade in a sense the poverty to which it was necessarily bound as natural speech. The rhetorical or persuasive conception of poetry prominent in the Middle Ages maintained its grip even with the rediscovery and dissemination of Aristotle's *Poetics* in the Renaissance, and the mimetic nature of poetry remained bound to the need to "edify" rather than simply describe. Poetry, in one influential sixteenth-century exposition, therefore involved the "faculty of finding out whatsoever is accommodated to the imitation of actions, passions, customs, in rhythmical language, for the purpose of correcting the vices of men and causing them to live good and happy lives."[28] Imitation, that is, for a more narrow purpose. Not that this purpose itself subverted imitation. But if the purpose of moral edification was to be rigorously pursued, it was obvious, then, that either poetry's relation to Nature would require circumscription, or that Nature herself would require reformation. Certainly Francis Bacon's famous reflection upon poetry as the inventor of "feigned histories" in order to provide the mind that "satisfaction . . . in those points wherein the Nature of things doth deny it" moves edification and nature on a collision course.[29] Later assimilators of the "classical" tradition of Aristotle and Horace, like Boileau, simply chose to stress the discerning need for choice mimetic "examples" rather than question the imitative purpose altogether.[30] This comes down to a kind of sentimental Platonism, one, some have noted, that is charged with a certain self-conscious cultural relativism, because "each age" will have its artificial forms through which pleasure is appropriately maintained. As with the ants, what is "natural" simply becomes a mirror to what is comfortable and already known.[31]

Nature, that is, is full of too many bad examples, and this recognition itself has blunted the easy application of an imitative Christian analogy.

28. B. Lombardus's Preface to the 1550 Italian edition of the *Poetics*, cited in Clark, *Rhetoric and Poetry in the Renaissance*, 103.

29. Francis Bacon, *Of [the Proficience and] Advancement of Learning* (1605), II.iv.2, cited from 1885 edition, 101.

30. See Boileau's *L'Art Poétique*, III.1ff., on how a little "artifice" can make the odious serpent pleasing. The point being, as he writes in a letter to Brossette in 1702, that "imitation should never involve too close a similarity to nature, otherwise the image will evoke as much horror as the original that is imitated." See Boileau-Despréaux, 61.

31. So, for instance, the well-studied topic of the eighteenth-century English garden as a reflection, not of "nature" any longer, but of the *genius loci* of its ethnic and regional context, wherein the natural world is tended in order to take the form of a people's local character. Cf. Hunt, *Figure in the Landscape*.

By contrast, and more pertinently to the meaning of such analogy, the Christian understanding of nature as the hard thing that stands from and apart from God, as creation even in its fallenness (and necessarily so in the present), represents an almost sullen tradition holding back the poetic vehicle of natural theology. One can view an aspect of Romantic naturalism as a coming to grief upon the reefs of such a Christian assertion, seeking after the outlines of the one "mind" behind both Books of God (Nature and the Bible), yet unwilling, usually, to accept the judgment of its shadows. The search for the essence of "Hebrew" poetry by someone like Robert Lowth was an honest quest, wherein the sublimity of the biblical writers still marked off the precincts of that within which the impoverished creation could not quite enter; but always there was a subterfuge, the discovery of a common Spirit between poet and reader, world and God, that somehow could overstep the bounds and render "bad examples" less troublesome through their moral applications—less troublesome, not for men and women, but for God's own Name, which is either glorified or blasphemed or simply unuttered among the nations. The fact that the Lives of Jesus, until perhaps Schweitzer's demotion of the genre, still described his humanity in nothing but the most docile (and later, fluidly persuasive) of terms marks out the subjugation of poetry still by an intuition that natural theology is an unsettling and unresolved pursuit, best compartmentalized and manipulated to the side of easier instincts.

For if we cannot look to the ants for wisdom, or if the wisdom that we find among the ants is not somehow their own, but taken from elsewhere, what shall we say of Jesus's own humanity? Whose is it? Speaking naturalistically and descriptively do we not find the shadows of his passage also somewhat dizzying? Not only do his words on mothers, fathers, and families, or his warnings of a violent end, but his commands, enough of them to be grouped by the critics as "hard sayings" for rich and poor alike, elicit incomprehension and reaction. These too are confrontative outlines, and therefore precisely the stuff of a natural theology, not so much as they are ordered in a dogmatic ethic, but just here, as our human perceptions of him bump up against the character of the divine, recoil, and hence speak to us of a God who has made us and is not ours first of all. Indeed, the natural history of such encounters and reactions defines one of the great domains of creation's theological analogy, not so much as to repudiate the God whom religion serves, but to speak to what the service of such a God has come to.

The natural theology of poetry, thus, has managed to find its way back into business through the writing of critical history. It is not quite as agile, this theology, because it is weighed down by the self-regard of methodologies and guild rivalries; but it marks the impossibility of evading description. To be sure, history does not become natural theology simply by placing a wedge between the story of the Christian Church and the "real God"—only individuals sin, according to such a perverted view, not the corporate truth of the *ecclesia* or the *electi*, or the Gnostic apprehenders of the Spirit—for this is to close one's eyes to natural knowledge itself. Yes, such a natural history of religion, which is the means of theology's appropriation of critical history, is and has proven deeply problematic for theology itself: in words attributed to Jules Renard, "I don't know if God exists; but it would be better for his reputation if he didn't." Nonetheless, the story of God's "reputation" is what natural religion provides us with, and it is a story with a tale to tell. Indeed—and Renard himself was entranced by "natural histories" of just the kind that theology ought to relish—natural religion provides us with "God's reputation" emblazoned on placards. The moral character of created religion is often used as a blunt weapon against God. Still—and here we are urged to recover our courage a bit as natural theologians—its full figure is usually left unexamined, with its yearning, anger, glory, despair and hope, vindictiveness, forgiveness gathered and scattered at once. For even when these are "left as they are," without the ordering of doctrine, yet even just as they are they display a world whose contours typify God. If poetry is the supreme art of imitation, it is now seen to be so in a way probably wholly unattractive to its classical theorists: it is *because* poetry is made up of scraps and threads of descriptive claims—this is the nature of verse as opposed to narrative prose—that it most "looks like" the world. But a world that is, by Christian definition, God's object.

And this, most especially, the Scriptures tell us over and over. They do so not only in books like Job, which has always been an attractive yet finally deeply unsatisfying instrument for natural theologians because its promises give way to something that is unresolved on its own terms. But from Genesis on, it is exactly the natural, even when broken down into the puckered bits of documentary fodder for the historians, that has both resolutely asserted itself and also proven so difficult as a divine indicator to modern theologians, whose response, like that towards the character of natural theology as a whole, has tended towards a certain Marcionitism: whatever resists framing the coherence of an acceptable divine morality must be split and separated. But it is just such coherence, in a basic and humanly apprehended sense, that natural theology, ordered by the outlines of the shadows that it pursues, will necessarily give up. This has been a weak point in theology as a whole: that is, that what Christians *say* about God, and how they display their faith, even and without flinching in their seeming contradictions, tells us something about God, analogously; just as the ants do, not so much as we record their logic, as when we grope after their concrete forms within time, and describe them, over and over, watching their passage out from God's strange wisdom. For God loves the ants in a special way. As Milosz writes in an early poem:

> The word Faith means when someone sees
> A dew-drop or a floating leaf, and knows
> That they are, because they have to be.
>
> And even if you dreamed, or closed your eyes
> And wished, the world would still be what it was . . .
>
> Look, see the long shadow cast by the tree;
> And flowers and people throw shadows on the earth:
> What has no shadow has no strength to live.[32]

And because of this shadow of obdurate presence, that itself informs our *faith*, we can affirm that to speak, even in such a difficult analogy, is to provide a "Christian natural religion" and from its study, a Christian natural theology.

NATURAL THEOLOGY AND CHRISTIAN CATEGORIES OF FAITH

If we pursue such speech as gives rise to such a natural theology, it will take the following forms. First, because such a theology is content to be mimetic, and in fact needs to remain so, it *will* be historical somehow. Hence, a part of a Christian natural theology is descriptive history; not a history recorded alone, but always within the context of Christian speech

---

32. Milosz, "Faith," from the longer poem "The World," in Milosz, *Separate Notebooks*, 143, 145.

that understands that such a history, however much it must turn in on itself, will bring into repute—some repute, dulled or blazoned, always as a shadow—the Name of God. And such a reputation may finally reflect upon the insulter rather than upon the Insulted.

The natural history of religion, then, will perform the task of *critically* hearing Christian speech: what do we grasp of God's outline, as it were, as Christians speak and act, and use words and gestures in such and such a way? There is an ascetic purpose to such hearing, a penitential one. But here we are aiming at another end. Nor will the goal of such a natural history simply be to understand the minds of specific Christians in time, but (which amounts to the same thing from one perspective) to see, as a Christian, how what we say and do runs us up against the very things we believe as we have been granted faith. In this way, historical study becomes theology because here we seek first to know God, not to reform ourselves (though we will wish to see this happen in our knowledge, surely). Moral commentators, then, are often the best natural theologians, as long as they are able to place themselves within the matrix of their own discussions descriptively and be, as it were, denuded with the crowd. Natural theology such as Paley practiced is therefore not so much to be rejected, but seen as only an initial step in such a work. For the next, the more fully historical one, demands an examination of Paley's moral philosophy and of his world, of Paley himself as he looked about and bent down to the ground and lifted up the ant, and sought him eye to eye. (And not Paley only, but any other Christian exponent whom one is studying—perhaps even one's own self as we dig up the posts for our fields.)

But the historical task gives rise to another and second form of study, one that, if followed through would mark this as a *useful* Christian natural theology, not simply in the edifying moral sense of classical *mimesis*, but in the truth-telling sense of religious metaphysics. And this second aspect would be to order this arrangement of morals and history, so to speak, within the constraining claims of the Christian faith itself. If God lived on earth, the Jewish proverb goes (in a way that turns Renand's claim into the worry of an anti-Semite), people would break his windows. And we are saying that the true God is, if not identical with, yet somehow analogous to the God not only aimed after by the window-breakers but at the same time sovereign over them. And we are saying this knowing that this God, whom the window-breakers (now extended not just to the anti-Semites but to all angry mobs and individuals) know only by reputation, also carries the reputation, that which we accept as in fact true, of being Father, Son, and Holy Spirit. So, this second form of natural theology is simply to place Jesus in the midst of these vying or even in some sense eliding reputations, and to search out in the outline's form his Name. So Blake writes: "Thinking as I do that the Creator of this world is a very cruel being, & being a worshipper of Christ, I cannot help saying: 'the Son, O how unlike the Father!' First God Almighty comes with a thump on the head. Then Jesus Christ comes with a balm to heal it."[33]

So Blake puts it, but of course debatably so in terms of his Christian conclusions (which are more Marcionite than true). Unlike the Scriptures, there is no canon to natural theology's investigations; poverty, like God, is limitless as well, in its negative curvature in relation to its Creator (who became "poor"!). That is why a natural theology *is* unresolved even in Christian terms, and does not simply stand as a second "book". It is instead an ongoing enunciation—as long as the world shall stand—not on its own, but as the descriptive counterpoint to the ongoing confession of the revealed claims of the Christian faith. Symbiotic in its integrity, Christian natural theology is a conscious, deliberate, and repeated bringing to bear of the encounter and juxtaposition of the natural world, including the human world, with the forms of Christian faith. The unity of *theologia naturalis* and *sacra doctrina* lies in the fact that this speech about the world's juxtaposition with the Gospel is what Christians say, over and over, as they look around themselves and into themselves: and if the Father and the Son thump heads and issue salves in the process, this is where the Trinity itself wrenches the mind of the believer, or even of the one coming to belief, into a truthful posture. The forms of the faith—the Apostles' Creed in the case of the present introduction—are, in a natural theology, those articulated elements that, as divinely given, cast their shadows on the world, alarming or protective as the case may be, and thereby in this consternation are inevitable aspects of the world's description underlined. It is not enough for the Christian to look at the world as thus shadowed; this is not sufficient for salvation. But it is a *necessary* thing to do, all the same, if we are to understand the form of the thing itself (and the Larkins and Weinbergs are right in their challenge)—the

---

33. William Blake, "A Vision of the Last Judgment," in *Complete Poetry and Prose of William Blake*, 565.

substance of that which casts its obscure outline, its weight, the volume of its reach—understand it and so be apprehended by it (1 Cor 13:12).

And it is here, in the shadowed world of the Creed's enunciation within space and time, uttered on the lips of those who break windows in more ways than one, that the peculiar character of Christian natural theology becomes apparent. The Platonist seeks only the form of God or of what is real, for the shadow is unsubstantial and partial. There is thus a Platonist bent to all the denigrators of natural theology as a Christian possibility and calling. So be it. But a less philosophically constrained, and in this sense truer and fuller, Christian apprehension will understand that God does *not* exist alone any longer, however much we must also assert that his being is "self-sufficient" despite our prayers that inundate his palaces; for precisely we know of God's self-giving in Christ Jesus through creation and in redemption, Christ Jesus the Son, gathered in His Spirit. Thus, to know God is to know God's shadows; or, even further, there is no God apart from the shadows that God casts; and yet again: to know God's shadows is indeed to know something that is fundamental to God that cannot be known apart from them. For "to see me is to see the Father" (John 14:9), says Jesus, the strange man who bleeds yet is risen. Yet through me "all things were made" and without me "was not anything made that was made" and I was "made flesh and dwelt" amid the world's men and women, rocks and beasts (John 1:3, 14). And the shadow of the Father is that which can say, "this is my Son" (Mark 9:7).

The metaphysical reticence, even strict self-limitation, in this kind of description of the relation between the "natural" and the "revealed" is deliberate. While there may be some kind of logical step, understood on levels aesthetic and philosophical, from nature to God, it is a step that historically cannot be taken on one's own, with one's eyes closed. If it happens, as it does, the step is always a wrenching away, whether we wish to dub it "natural" or "gracious". That too is a part of its logic.[34]

---

34. These are passionately fought theological issues, probably never capable of satisfactory articulation. See Murphy, *Christ the Form of Beauty*, for a subtle discussion of competing modern and Catholic approaches that (*contra* Barth's worries over the latter's naturalism) demonstrates the particular and necessary power of scriptural revelation as the ground of nature's indicative power.

Ephraim Radner

THE THEOLOGICAL NECESSITY OF POETRY

Although natural theology implies poetry, and calls it forth, it does not ask nor does it demand a specific kind of poetry. In fact, the encounter of Christian speech with the outlines of the world's description that marks the center of natural theology is necessarily *un*restrictive in this work: the world is described in its diversity, which means only in bits and pieces—hence the scraps of versification and their threading together—while the words of revelation speak in their specific form, which requires, at least over time and in their grand narrative, a systematic focus of enunciation. But the two sides of the encounter cannot be equivalent in form. What is generally called "religious poetry," therefore, will likely fail in its lack of naturalism, while poetry, standing alone as it were, does not become a usable theology until it is questioned with the very words of Christ.

But what is "naturalism" in this context? Is it a particular subject matter? Certainly, it is not the same as a hymn, of a kind that seeks to explain in verse some Christian truth that is mimetic only with respect to the grammar of its referent. Some hymns, still in use in our churches, are by contrast naturalistic in their description of Christian experience (e.g., Cowper) or of the world that is touched and transfigured by that truth itself (e.g., Smart). So we might say that subject matter is perhaps important up to a point, insofar as description remains a goal (and there are certainly other goals to be had).

In this vein the writer and scholar Jonathan Bate recently made an eloquent plea for the recovery of the natural in poetry.[35] Bate is after something more than the bare description of the "natural world," but certainly not wholly other than this. Indeed, he is after, in his own way, something that natural theology has rightly aimed after as well and sought to uphold: the necessary identification and indwelling of externalities by human beings. Still, it is necessary to note where a plea like Bate's both succeeds and fails in terms of a Christian natural theology. Positively, he is able to locate the proper character of creation as a shadow: "the poetic articulates both presence and absence: it is both the imaginary recreation and the trace on the sand which is all that remains of the wind itself. The poetic is ontologically double because it may be thought of as ecological in two senses: it is either (both?) a language (*logos*) that restores us to our home

---

35. Bate, *Song of the Earth*, especially the concluding chapters, 203–83.

Introducing an Introduction to Christian Natural Theology

(*oikos*) or (and?) a melancholy recognizing that our only home (*oikos*) is language (*logos*)."[36] This is right: the finitude of our language, captured by the creature's need for God, yes, who is and remains *unlike* the natural world, displays to us the truth.

It is also the case, however, that the *oikos* of "ecology" cannot simply be a world that is other than human altogether, and that somehow stands as the human being's own "lost" innocence and is that ever against which humanity stands at best ambiguously. That is to replace God with Nature as the great Alterity—moving beyond Spinoza to Hegel in at least a small compass—and to confuse the ecology and households of the world with that of grace. Since it *is* the "universal poverty" that is at issue in any Christian natural theology, what is "natural" and divinely outlined and othered includes even the artifacts of human life itself, cast in with the beasts and ants, all of it living to the far side of God who has somehow for reasons hidden in the divine heart made them live beside and other to him. This is where Bate's adoption of a *jejeune* and all too common notion of Christianity's "depreciation" of the natural world as a "creation"[37] points up a central aspect of natural theology: the proper position of human life is one with the beasts amidst creaturely construals of the world. It cannot be that *God's* life with us is what makes us forgetful even of God's works and of his being towards them. Indeed, to claim otherwise—that is, that God is the source of our estrangement from the world—is to demand of poetry what it cannot give. It is, as Bate seems to wish, inappropriately to elevate poetry, broadly understood, into a vatic realm of ghostly medium, the one thing that can perhaps save us, rather than allowing it to stand as what it is in fact, a starkly unadorned but not unique instance of speech that, because it is essentially bound to the natural, speaks only of the shadowed world as a whole. It is also to keep poetry from doing just that, indicating God along with and through its bondage to the world as God's *creature*. For if the artifacts of humanity are not themselves "natu-

---

36. Ibid., 281.

37. Ibid., 256, quoting from Heidegger's seminars on Hölderlin's hymns, translated by Bruce V. Foltz, in Foltz, *Inhabiting the Earth: Heidegger, Environmental Ethics, and the Metaphysics of Nature*, 63: "Once through Christianity, whereby nature was, in the first place, depreciated to [the level of] 'the created', and at the same time was brought into a relation with super-nature (the realm of grace)." Bate draws this into relation to other "radical ecological" critiques of Christianity, like Lynn White Jr.'s.

ral," they are given the false office of the magical. Poetry is all too human, and hence natural enough itself to be a willing trace.

And poetry is at its best when, therefore, it works as the incisive catalogue of naturalism, for the sake of clear outlines, and then simply lays its forms at the precipice of its descriptions, within the roar of Scripture's cataracts. The Objectivist impulse, as seen in the pure forms of something like the early Charles Reznikoff, provides the necessary base for such a poetry. But Reznikoff's later Scriptural containers and encounters, from a Jewish perspective, show also this model's necessary theological fulfillment.[38] Without this Scriptural encounter, naturalism develops its own religious, and often idolatrous, imagination.[39] In its encounter with the larger realm of God's life, given in Scripture most fully, poetry itself can never systematize the natural forms provided it, it can only look and, if sufficiently focused, gaze, with the blunted epiphanies of St. Jerome, in James Wright's late poem: "To see the lizard there,/ I was amazed I did not have to beat/ My breast with a stone . . . I was not even / Praying, unless: no, / I was not praying . . . But he did not move./ Neither did I./ I did not dare to."[40]

If lizards were somehow more fruitful in their stillness, more profoundly referring, more transfiguring of vision, they too would arm the idols. But their inner corridors, however vast, give no way out. So too the words that speak of them; otherwise they will destroy precisely the shadowed and thereby indicative character of these forms. Just as the world cannot order itself, its persistent disorder must be preserved if only to speak truthfully of its nature, however necessary the Scriptural light may be to bring it to disclosure.

---

38. See the new edition of Reznikoff's complete shorter poems, that captures the movement and, from the perspective of theology, deepening development of his work: *The Poems of Charles Reznikoff. 1918–1975*.

39. Cf. Robert Bly's anthology *News of the Universe*. The subtitle of the anthology, "Poems of Twofold Consciousness," expresses the particular direction Bly will press his collection of often otherwise pristinely naturalistic exemplars, ordered according to a carefully wrought New Age religious vision that he articulates through a series of illustrative essays. By contrast, an anthology like Czeslaw Milosz's *A Book of Luminous Things* takes in a range of material very similar to Bly's in form, but leaves it, as it were, just as it is found and read, and at least preserves the reader's own possible Scriptural encounter.

40. Wright, "Jerome in Solitude," in Wright, *Above the River*, 365.

Poetry, then, even as Scripturally informed, cannot dogmatize, just as the world cannot be certain of anything other than its own transience. It cannot reveal, but only indicate from its distance as the world's far speech. Poetry certainly cannot save, for it, along with its world, utters the cry that requires saving. Poetry's usefulness, indeed its supreme usefulness to natural theology lies just in the way it embodies each of these elements in a clear and formal way, its own technical constraints demanding that it keep to this purpose, its own versifying consigning to the limits of this purpose. It is the one haphazard discipline that is thus perfectly adapted to and expressive of the world. And in doing so, poetry is useful as the edge against which Christian speech in its revealed grace finds its own form in the world. For Christian speech, coming in the wake of Christ, cannot exist in a divine vacuum apart from the world's forms.

Any natural theology, even one seeking to persuade like Paley's, will take the world as it is found and, without translation, allow the Scriptures and the Church to speak to and with it. It is not so much that some essential congruence will be thereby disclosed, although it is surely there; rather, such congruence as there is will be discovered, not simply asserted, which is where the givenness of world and revelation find their human meaning. In the introduction that follows, the words of the Creed—revealed, in an ecclesial sense, as Scripture's verse—order each of the poetic artifacts that are gathered in their shadow. The artifacts themselves might well stand alone, as all things can seem to do in the world, ordered variously and impermanently, and certainly obscurely. But here they take their descriptive contents, which even when speaking of a high and developed faith as much as of the ants, stand at the edge of the precipice to the side of God, and let His day pass by, whether before or behind, as in a crevice marked by the shadows of his glory. This is an explicit example of a more pervasive and necessary reality: that every time the world is described poetically by the Christian, that world utters the words of the Creed, not wholly, not fully, not with complete understanding; but the words nonetheless are formed and enunciated, and are filled with air and become sound, so that it is true that "their sound is gone out into all lands: and their words into the ends of the world" (Ps 19:4, Book of Common Prayer).

In what follows, written over the course of a number of years, natural theology is pursued through the simple and discrete practice of describing the world—poetry—as a place where the words of the Christian

Creed are enunciated. This is to say—which is the deep saying of all that human beings make along with all that stands within and beside them, turning to the Lord of Heaven and Earth, the Father of Jesus Christ, and the giver of all Life—this is to say: "You made me!"

The Apostles' Creed

I believe in God, the Father Almighty
    Creator of heaven and earth.

I believe in Jesus Christ, His only Son, our Lord,
    He was conceived by the power of the Holy Spirit
        and born of the Virgin Mary.
    He suffered under Pontius Pilate,
        was crucified, died, and was buried.
    He descended to the dead.
    On the third day he rose again.
    He ascended into heaven
        and is seated at the right hand of the Father.
    He will come again to judge the living and the dead.

I believe in the Holy Spirit,
    the Holy Catholic Church
    the communion of saints
    the forgiveness of sins,
    the resurrection of the body,
    and the life everlasting. Amen.

1. I

How shall an old man
mend his ways?
Perhaps, like the starling
who moves too quickly from up high

and swoops against
the clear pane,
lying stunned
for cat or for coyote to discover,

maybe to revive,
shaking its head,
rolling over
for another, smaller, shorter day.

Perhaps, again,
by sitting behind
the counting table
summing up the loss of children, outliving

their laughter, their resentments,
their white teeth,
their long hair,
stacking up the worthless coin.

Better yet,
someone can rise up
behind him, speaking
truth where before the words had taken on

Ephraim Radner

a sing-song hum
of haggard verse,
but now new speech
will quiet old tongues and blinking eyes.

But best of all would be
the simple change
wherein the skin turns in
upon itself
fold upon fold, each wrapping
the shrinking form
with tightened, gentle plates
that rise and fall
with every passing breeze,
green and lithe
the eyes now swollen with light,
the legs bent
the wings carefully readied,
the fields open,
chanting, chanting softly
as you enter
Aurora's cool halls.

2. Believe

He bores through the tree,
turning it ashen in a season,
every corridor, run to its end,
the beetle's glory.

A thousand eggs,
housed, glistening in corners
of the earth, waiting for light.
It arrives on time.

And the ants, ever sage,
food stacked away for summer,
badgers among stones, and lizards
on kings' thrones?

They know nothing!
I roam heaven's tree,
give birth to a million thoughts,
crave and thirst.

My instinct is God,
driven, the world ringing
with passions, striving, and I
am wise too.

3. In

A small confession first:
that although I am afraid
of falling,
I have pangs
exhilarating gut to eye
that catch me staring out at what is swallowed from below.

My room would disappear,
spin around the pages opened
to mastodons—
they deserved it,
crying in the tar
up to their waists now;
then quiet but for the
sound of its grip.

A thrill prickled the laughter
and clung about the walls
when I read aloud to them,
"whole tractors lost,
no trace of men building
railroad in Siberian mud."

Or campfire songs,
hearty, forced, possessed
by the singing
of *Titanics*
and every other boat
celebrated on shore
for staying out and giving in.

The World in the Shadow of God

    I admit to the summers,
    the stern drawn-out obsession
    by the lake,
    tossing stones
    far into the water
    where they are lost to the eye,
    waiting for the ripples to return.

4. God

I.

If God were finally gotten rid of,
then the sacrifices that we did, on
earth and altars, cooked and slit . . .
No, meat would live! and families sit
in lovely grass. We would have picnics,
holidays! Where is the sickness
in the air? Accordions play
their dandelion tunes. We slay
only the vine today. The sun
is mating. Why so sad? So glum?
Why then the looks so long, so deep?
Jump now, yell out loudly, whistle, leap.

A blessed grace of fancy:
to have chosen distant dancing
as you contemplate—besotted,
bloodless, barren—where no God is.

II.

In every rock lies the realm of the living.
Had Moses patience, had Israel given
up her craving for a moment,
when the waters gushed and foamed,
they might have seen the teeming ants
within, around the table, hands
about the cup, arranged in ranks,
each of them chanting thanks.

Each day, each following rock, each flame
for Israel—deep inside the frame
of each, yet further still, inside
the scurrying limbs: more tables, wide
and long, more bread at every seat,
more purring wings, more songs, more feet.

Oh Moses, look inside the mountain
when its top is shook, its sounding
summit blazing, trumpet blasts
again announcing that at last
the contents of the promised hill
are bared for the stars to see, the stilled
heavens to wrap, and peace relentlessly
to hold: they are all swarming, and the endless
tables filled. Look! They sing
inside night's atoms, inside of things
that are not yet, inside of even
death itself, inside the seasons
of a Time not marked, nor said, nor known—
the whirring, pressing, tingling of stones.

Ephraim Radner

III.

The closet opens to the dark.
In the farthest corner,
where the boards are worn from sitting,
from rubbing hands and cheeks,
repeating the words and charges,
everything is gathered
in piles ringing his feet.

In the closet's darkness
lies a remarkable
box, to the side of his feet.
In it is the dust and rock
of all the world, resting,
gathered, mixed
with the people's harsh words.

The closet is dark and secret.
He gathers his knees
to his chin here, seeing
secretly, hiding the piles,
rubbing his cheek against
the wall, sensing
all the words and their edges.

How did the world become
a secret? How hid,
put away meekly, nested
in a box, laid in a corner,
made small, yet suffusing the walls?
How held tight
in the greatest quiet of all?

IV.

When the children sang their song, they did not know;
they did not know of what would come
in the year ahead.

Their notes were pure and high, and on they flowed,
embracing earth and air with a young,
piercing light that fed

the deep and sped past planes above,
that made the silken surface bristle,
while pressing down into the core.

They sang, but did not know about the rough
bulrushes where their parents, missiles
flying, will crouch in horror,

while men will hunt them down with clubs and knives,
while water laps against their knees
and they bend down low.

They did not know that in a year, their wise
teachers will slip away and flee,
and the schools will be emptied and closed.

They did not know how the churches will be filled,
but the prayers inside will be hemmed in
and beaten about the head.

They did not know about the camp, its hills
covered by tents, swelling, tending
thousands, living and dead.

Ephraim Radner

None of this they knew when they sang that day.
Yet the song they sang knew all, somehow.
It somehow knew it well,

like the light tightening its grip far into space,
like blood bristling and bursting now
with a desire that presses and swells,

like the wind that clears the surfaces, howls and one day
reaches the halls of a distant land
where someone pauses and wonders.
(Great Lakes Region, 1990–2009)

5. The Father

I.

A man asked his boy,
"What is the most beautiful thing in the world?"
"Stars at night,
when they are falling."

"Then what is the saddest thing you know?"
"It's when a child is lost and weeps."
The man asked,
"Do stars have children?"

For he wondered at the shape
of beauty and its infant cries.
He thought to himself,
Is it like

the water in a stream
which from its icy start flows down
past rocks and woods,
the first drop gone

into a long sigh
that stretches past the ear and memory?
Is it like
the reddish sand

that tops the towering hills,
because below are centuries of stone
still giving birth,
though no one knows?

"Will you be lost as well?"
"Perhaps", the boy replied. "And will it
be forever?"
"O Lord, you know."

The World in the Shadow of God

II.

He left his hair uncut
for days. Nothing was piled
on the platters served around.
When the clouds hung over,
borne up on the branches, he was
tied at the head.

Arms were given out,
green against his hair
stroking the shadows of his hair
with darts of light just as
those curls and glinting blades
that wave in the branches.

The leaves held him through
to the end of his straining head,
stretched to serve around;
saved for the rocks,
for shouting—for "Absalom!"—
for the nation's ruddy health.

Between heaven and earth
are shadows and clear shafts
saving as he wriggles,
as a tree among trees presses
Judah's soil through its toes
until the earth is rooted.

Ephraim Radner

This is the steady rule
for all the corners of creation:
pick and choose the order,
have the prophets mutter
a name or two,
be subtle or crude—one man
must still die for the nation.

6. Almighty

I.

It is all a kind of scratching
in the dirt for dirty metaphors,
this vain obeisance:
veins on leaves
crackling with fragility;
watching eyes that glow upon
the wings of winter moths
dissolving under the dew;
the steady grasp of roots
sufficiently sucking up their need;
and the like.

Here is a culled particular:
I saw a miraculous march
of ants this morning,
the small ones
round like pellets of grain,
moving their loads
in one direction,
visible only
as they crossed my path.
Above them, arched
in a rickety scaffolding
of small *carceri*
were arrayed the thousands
of bodyguards, bit
thugs of black pinchers
with a mass of spindly legs
dipped in red poison.

Ephraim Radner

Then, to the side prowling
up to my feet roved
the watchmen, ever-ready
with their prodding filaments.
This is the third day
they are marching.

I will seek them out tomorrow
to test analogy.
Destined like our world
to move into God's hands
with all the glorious traces
of the tending, reaching globe:
so marches too our fantasy,
in one direction,
beautiful and gentle
as these mindless lines
are driven by the mathematics
of their honed percentage.

Order has no thought,
we have been taught.
As with the clouds
thrown up against the pressing sky,
the rain comes without warning.
Paths are cleared again.
Purpose is perhaps
the special color of a beast.
But endless power,
empty to our eyes,
must wash the sense away.

II.

We all lay down on time—
the smoke and grime gone up
like perfumed peace
consumed on a table that stretches
far beyond the hem of the world.

There rests a child's nation,
carefully stationed and measured.
I lived there;
shivered at night in bed;
looked out at the waiting moon.

I walked the country's length;
I grew in strength and passed
the idle toying,
side by side in the sun,
turning white, slowly, on the stones.

Some cities were rebuilt,
some of the wilted skies;
a few fields,
now yielding a hundred-fold
to red hands like my own.

We would slap each other,
a firm touch lasting
before the cold
roared through with its frost
that chewed friendships to stubble.

Ephraim Radner

Then we tackled the whole land,
banded around the head
to soak up our sweat;
dangling in the wind
we said goodbye as it dried.

7. Creator

I.

Today there are clouds,
yesterday none.
Tomorrow we will count them
one by one.
Somewhere in the middle someone
bravely strives to tell the sky;
but taken by the vastness
of the space between, she's lost.
God is just.
For He is eminently pleased by this,
His work.
So must we be by His.

Today there is talking,
yesterday none.
Tomorrow we shall hear each sound
one by one.
Somewhere in the middle, someone
stands to resonate the strands that bind the vastness
of the space between. He falls.
God is just.
He is still eminently pleased by this
His work.
So must we be by His.

Today there is sweat,
yesterday none.
Tomorrow droplets fly by
one by one.
Somewhere in the middle someone
holds his hands within the folds

that tie the vastness
of that space between these days.
God is just,
His ways made eminently pleased by this
His work.
So must we be by His.

Today there's a story,
yesterday none.
Tomorrow and beyond
they will be done.
Somewhere in the middle somewhere
we are all arranged, floating
in between the numbered labors
of our years, so vast
that God is surely just,
at least to be so eminently pleased by this,
His work.
So must we, must we be by His.

The World in the Shadow of God

II.

Solomon places his ear to the ground,
attempting to glean any trace of a sound.
The ants are marching two by two,
and Solomon, the king of the Jews,

is ready to order them all to reveal
the secrets of how they manage to deal
with wind and rain, with torrents of mud,
that for Jews necessarily end in their blood

spilled over the banks and bodies broken.
Yet the ants never mourn, no prayer's ever spoken.
they have no Temple; they sing no hymns;
they do not sacrifice for sins.

"I asked that God would make me wise!",
says Solomon, and standing he cries,
"But wisdom teaches that between ant and the man
the difference lies in that the man can

do nothing but pray when the land starts to heave,
do nothing but sing when the people all grieve,
do nothing but wail for the ills they have done,
while the ant merely crawls back out with the sun."

And if the sun itself were to never appear?
Solomon again knelt down, with his ear
cocked to the ants. "Still I would hear
nothing, nothing, year after year."

Ephraim Radner

"I am wise", says the king. "Between me and the ant
a chasm is placed, and only God grants
a bridge that can reach, that will join up the two."
Gentiles, not ants, says the Lord of the Jews.

The World in the Shadow of God

III.

There are nothing but things—
grand and small,
clinging, toppling, bumping, grasping,
standing and naked
thumping and crying out,
shaking the sky in great towers.
I try, but within them am lost.

There are only rocks.
Who shall go through them?
Stones that roll on and on,
crackling and strewn
so that we are always digging.
How shall I or even you get back
from under their thick layers?

What else but pots,
stacked and clattering?
With every stuttering and drunken fall
the ears slacken;
with spilling and smothered calls,
black pans, outpouring the cupboards for years,
where shall we put our food?

There are nothing but things,
lashed onto the pyres,
too many even for the fires to bring
down into ashes.
Instead, they are jealously hoarded
by the light that has found their edges, that enters
in, that glows and roars.

Ephraim Radner

There are only the happenings
of all these things,
the mapping of their rumblings and demise,
of their coming and going.
O Grand Materialist! Whose size
is moated and bound, yet running even
to the far light of other eyes!

8. Of Heaven

With one quick sweep
he drew a line across the sky,
placing the sun and heat in the midst,
the color red rubbed from end to end.
The heavens were a desert now,
untended, grainy, dried by time,
whittled with small lives,
invisible, searched after.

Declare my glory!, he said.
The universe was vastly quiet.
Forever and ever, it seemed,
but for the sounds of distant,
innumerable scratchings.

9. And Earth

I.

At five, the wind runs down the road.
From there it wraps the live oaks in its arms,
throwing sound out to the grasses, quelling
birds, upending stones.
Beneath them are the eyes, the eyes of the Prophets

from whom the cloudless air takes sight.
Out towards the edge, the edge of the hills,
the crests of the grasses, from there to the ocean below,
crouch bushes. They have hands,
not roots; the hands of the dead, waving towards

the leaves behind them, the angels' hair,
from whose long strands we think of endless hope.
They flatten with the wind, their heads deep set
inside the soiled globe,
inside, with swarms of lights and calls and joys.

For the earth is full of wondrous things—
inside, the Testaments, in stone and blood,
from whom the names of all the plants are writ,
and oil in shining vats,
from which the universe anoints its hymns.

II.

I had a gentle baby,
bristling as a boar
that runs, with great and gleaming hooves,
across the wooden floor.

The child now lies buried,
struck by a hunter's dart,
her warm and glistening silver fur
cut deeply to the heart.

I had another child.
She leapt up like a deer
who, frightened in the forest light,
is rushed by brazen spears.

The last young that I bore,
had eyes that sparkled red
as foxes' tails that lie against
The snow, when they are dead.

My children had no names.
For God gave out this work
to Adam, who, in earths' dark sod,
is sod's most gentle clerk.

Ephraim Radner

III.

For thirty years, at her window's perch
she watched the men as they went to work.
Her own had gone and not come back
one day long ago; it was a black
memory. But others carried on,
almost marching with their pails, young, married.
"It's beautiful", said Ada; "men working,
going, coming, with a purpose, sturdy.
It's glorious!". Even the trucks in line,
rumbling along, which shook the china.

One day, years from now, they would find
in the rubble of a field, in a mound, mined,
covered with grass, the bits of china,
with its blue designs, faded and grimy.
Perhaps the pit of a tribe, whose banks
had long since moved and dried, the ranks
of mangroves withered, the fish bones ground.
Their women carried babies, pounded
roots , the men folk speared and traded;
the Dutch were everywhere, seedy and faded.

The men who work are beautiful, and toil
is like the air, like the grass, like the soil
that washes back and forth across
the continents, its shifting waves tossing
spume that gleams at each revolving:
the sun arousing or the night resolving.

IV.

Coney, coney, in your hole
of dirt and stone: the wind has rolled
the clouds above your straining head
that watches lest the daily bread
of hawk and kite the Lord will grant
makes you their gift. His open hand,
as seasons run, will feed
each beast: today are seeds;
tomorrow all will turn to ice
at dawn. What will you do? With mice
and hare you'll sink into the earth.
Coney, coney, who is first
among the creatures? Hawk or kite,
as you sleep through the winter's night?
Only the stars now set their sights
on food, gnawing bits of light.

10. I Believe In

For those who wish to know the truth,
wish like Bruno for the truth,
sainted in the wilds, where the fire
is clear and dark beasts brood:

a wolf ate Bruno's flesh one day.
It took his flesh to dine that day.
Yet God restores the joints and makes them whole
that we might learn to pray.

The winter wrapped the rocks with cold,
all that it touched was wrapped in cold.
while Bruno froze and turned to aching blue
God cloaked his cracking soul

with prayer. A bear came out and grew
into the whispering night, he grew
into the cell that Bruno kept, and grasped
him hard. The soul is true

that a brown bear grips. And fire,
when it drives such bears away, a fire
that God has lit across the mountain peak's
pocked, jagged side, will tire

out the beasts. For Bruno seeks
the tongue within; the flame he seeks
must lap the forest groves and bears
without, but let love leak

The World in the Shadow of God

within. God bursts his hill such days;
The mountains smoke and churn such days.
The earth and all her beasts gave Bruno way
that he might learn to pray.

This is the truth that saints must know.
Beneath the cliffs we too must know
that the beasts and fire that drive our prying cries
one day are slowed.

11. Jesus Christ

My mind has handled many things
that neither earth nor heaven shall bring
to me. Nor does God wish it so.

On empty nights I sit low
on the mat; my heart begins to pound,
my eyes grow large, as if I've found
their touch finally.

I shall never taste a boiled
egg, a full-grown chick with oily,
tender feathers curled inside.

Across in Egypt, I might have tried
such food. But I'll have raised the dead
without once even these tiny heads
caressing my throat.

How many times, lying alone
I've donned a silken suit that shone
with the deep blue of a trading man

from Sheba posing with a fan,
covered by its rippled threads
of white garland and birds, their red
beaks darting

like flakes of water on my back;
the cloth would stroke my flesh, tracking
in up my legs, then flowing down.

But as I lay now upon the ground
like a brown sack, the suit is burning
many miles away, turning
into mind's ash.

I have swayed masses with my talk,
pounding my fist, thousands walked
to my insistence, stretching their souls.

We'd have built a new nation from the old.
My hands knew it. In the square
I've slept on benches that the sun's air
flooded with joy.

After dark, I turned in at
a Greek hotel. The maids all sat
beside me, pouring new wine while

they kissed my cheek. Beasts and mild
children, they've nudged up to my side
gently. And I, a gentle guide
to them. I thrilled.

I bound the wounds of lepers. I knew
their names: Sarah, Leah, a rude
and eyeless man named Barnabas.

We ate, we sang as one, for I was
family, made by love. My God
was glad. The tale that I had brought
I lived to tell.

I was driven on by hope
so as to be a cause of unbroken
amazement. My Father was glad indeed.

Ephraim Radner

Meanwhile, Desire came to feed,
to slip me, as I waited on
the morning's peace, faint drops of dawn's
light moisture.

She squeezed a spoon into my lips,
then drew me forward in small fits
and starts, rubbing the cold out

of my joints. Each time Desire bowed
to me. But we shall never wed.
Death leaves no taste, as I've often said
to children.

And they are mourning kids I live among—
so hungry, each, and still so young
that Desire's basket seems an ample

gift. God tells me: share some samples
with them; divvy up the bread
that pours out on the ground; get
some piece for them

to suck on back at home. I say
to them—for I am dying, day
by day, spurned by my wants—

I say to them, as they all hunt
amid the pile of crumbs that is spread
in front—I've always said—I say:
Eat what's been given.

12. His

My neighbor's chickens,
white, clouds of white
up to the neck
where their ugly faces
take off—
they were boudoir soft
and white if you closed your eyes to their faces,

if you closed your eyes,
with your hands, only your hands
against the white,
where their awkward bodies
could fly,
if ever they could fly . . .
and if you closed your eyes
you could finger their passage.

As if their passage
were in robes, satin robes
smelling of oils
from steaming baths;
as if your mother,
emerging from the bathroom,
in soft, white robes,
finally embraced you,

and the feathers embraced you,
waves, waves against your skin,
even as you held on.
"Mine", she muttered.
These hens,
my neighbors told me,
amid the night waves,
had smothered their chicks.

And the chicken man,
pretending, only pretending—
no woman he—
to own his young,
to hold them,
let drop Jerusalem,
in unending love,
where the dust still settles.

13. Only Son

The cats were hungry too.
They had waited through the various acts
by the Theater of Marcellus.
Pagans, Christians, Jews
in faith's twisted progression
had made of them the final players.

Since I had walked so long
just to step over their thronging sighs,
past a Roman kosher butcher
whose broken glass had strong
tape binding its name,
I excused myself into a side

alley. There were curtains
hiding the work and heavy air
inside of a restaurant.
I hate eating where
the sin of my solitude is seen
in public, so I quietly went in.

With no one else to serve,
the unhurried waiter brought cold
soup, thin veal, and then
a single orange, alone
on a plate. I peeled it first
before gently slicing, to exaggerate

Ephraim Radner

the time I had before me.
In three pieces, instead of trying
for the usual, tired four,
I sucked the juice and seeds.
Then one slipped out on the floor,
glistening down where it had dripped.

We stopped, the waiter towered
over where the sour
pip lay dropped on the deserted ground.
Our glances remained cowering
beside the flashing spot
which lay between our eyes.

14. Our Lord

I.

I am in a city, on some small
alleyway. The dust is visible in the sunlight.
I stop before a cobbler's stall, which is covered
with small silver bells. Every blow he strikes
and the alley jingles.
"Your feet are too small, anyway,"
he sneers at me, and goes back to jingling.
I pick up a sandal, examine it, and then
suddenly, I am beating him over the head
with this piece of ill-sized leather.
He laughs at me. "They are still too small!",
he says, and I look down at my feet:
shrunken, like a child's, barely able
to carry my weight.
"New shoes!", the cobbler taunts and jingles,
"New shoes for you!"

II.

I am walking through a plain.
It must be Spring, for the air is light
but warm. There are small white flowers
everywhere. I come to a great,
amber mountain, all in a shadow,
rising from the fields.
Crowds surround it. Everyone is pushing,
their breath is fetid.
"You must stand in line!", they shout
at me. "Is it long?", I ask.
"It will be very long indeed," they cry.
I complain: "But the mountain is already burning."
"Yes, it is at that." They all agree, shift their feet and spit
violently.

15. He Was Conceived

I saw God passing by the other day
beneath a large umbrella. For the men
above were raining down on him. True, some, when
hitting, fell with bitter thuds. He braved
their weight, then overstepped them on the paved
walkway. But most joined in the spotless spin
of sighs onto his soaking coat and thin
footsteps. He shivered softly, pulled his gray
scarf tight, and plodded on, as if for an
appointment. Yes, the chimneyed house ahead
was hers. He paused in front, and after one
cold fumbling try he entered, coat undone,
feet still un-wiped, umbrella fully spread.
I looked for rising smoke, but there was none.

16. By

All things break.
Their little heap is easily seen
in the center of the room.

There are my nails,
bent, cracked, picking at teeth,
whose bits still glitter too.

Do you remember the fall?
You took it flat on the nose. It's there.
And you were eighty-two.

The car sputtered,
the bridge collapsed; it was play
of course . . . the first time.

I was rummaging—
pulled that out, along with
a hopeless hat. Really.

Rakes, elbows,
swimming trunks (all striped!),
an enormous burnt cake-tin

filled with crumbs
from the walls—after all these years—
like the shards of imploded gears.

Shoe-laces, ropes,
the biggest lever I have ever seen—
if you could find the other pieces.

The World in the Shadow of God

That was the time
we lifted over a thousand boxes
from one place to another.

You tore your dress,
but the sweat felt good, didn't it,
streaking the dust on your face.

And when you cried,
it was as if your eyes melted
in pools. They're somewhere here.

Enough said.
This sorting out is a tiring business,
which makes me stop for breath.

Nothing works;
Besides—it's a kind of rapturous embrace
where nothing need be fixed.

17. The Power

To be a widow has its finer points.
The lively, grating talk is gone for good.
Meals are simple, and when you awake
on brilliant mornings after all the rain
has swept through, the clouds still scooping out
the sky with no restraint, your body tingles,
and at last, the tingle is alone.

God became a widow just last week,
I heard and thought of sending some kind words.
But I knew that her hair would now be lying
loose, her pale skin in the mirror finally
brightening as it caught the hazy gray
of dawn. I knew the sigh would send out peace—
peace—that in the end the trees would cease
from growing and from falling, that the streams
would freeze without an ice. I knew that in
the end the cracks would still the surface of
the globe, would stand forever—and not us.

God has a comb, and wondrous hands to hold it.
So I shall wait until she steps outside
before I dare approach with any boldness.

18. Of the Holy Spirit

Lord come, unclothe me.
Lay the folds outside the door.
Take my skin as yours
then lead me in where light cannot enter,
but will, when once my heart is mixed
into your hidden potion,
spilt, seep out the floor.

19. Born

The secret that you whispered in the night
you asked to have me wrap up in the dawn's
faint shadow. You said, "Throw it in the yawning
gap between my voice and flesh." Now light,
you stood and shouted at me what I shunned
that moment of my waking. Head and limbs,
you beat about with all your strength. The sin
of seeing you is blasted with the sun.
At evening you then urged, "Hide what you've gazed
upon. Let every eyelash fade and vision
drift, so that my ancient skin is misted
air, pale flakes only a late wind raises."
Thus you made the day too loud and all
the rest a time too soft to hush its fall.

20. Of the Virgin Mary

There was a woman
who received five wishes.
But with the first
she was very rash
And took all she thirsted after.

With the next four,
she lost it bit
by bit so that there
was only little left
to her in the bare house.

In the end she ran
outside on a hill,
where she wildly cursed
her luck. She filled
the sky with a skittish wind.

It was thin like her hair
and dismal thoughts
which rustled even
the trees. It brought
to mind a grieving sense of

"I am left to myself."
Yet God passed by
in a blowing mist.
He lifted high
her fingers, and he kissed them

Ephraim Radner

with His lips.
She stood in the flying
grass and raised
her hands in the air.
They were luminous and amazing.

21. Suffered

I took what illumined
and found it hard.
So I gave it to my God.
He rolled it in
His empty hand
then beat it with a rod.

He cast it into
the water's reach,
which tossed it high and swayed
the thing; then thrust up
on the beach,
God carried on the play.

God handed it back
and slyly said
that what is mine must be
always mine and
always mine. And
this is the hardest to see.

22. Under

I.

One humiliating thing
when you live within a belly
is having to wash
your hair in the evil-smelling
juices of your host.

Or always side-sliding
out from one membrane
to another
every time the vain
master takes movement

into his own hands.
The darkness here holds
you in a different,
sickly way, folding
gelatin around your face.

Shaking off disgust
for a moment, there are the good
points: such as everything
is soft; no metal, wood,
or plastic arrows that jut

out at inopportune times,
as in the world alas.
All the bumps are cushioned in a mass
of strawberry down (I think—

the light is fickle here).
To be able to see clearly!
But rising and falling,
the exercise grows weary
in this insulated ocean,

where safety is a prison.
I can imagine you—
"greater than Jonah!"—
below my tragic view,
racing underneath

the whale's dyspepsia.
But from there the sight spreads,
magnificent;
the lines stretch, threads
of lambent flickering,

towards the front and the rear
of a dissolving water light.
A kind of lamprey
to the flowing depths and heights,
you minister with loosened hair,

you stream through currents,
your face observes the truth
of each escape
and plunges beneath the roof
set above the whole.

You have the power to be crushed
or thrown against the lowest
unseen rocks.
What will pain you most
is the freedom to be lost,

Ephraim Radner

unexpectedly.
Chance, the sea, tides
rolling and pulling—
it is also a secret ride
that one day might float clear,

clear of the whole mess,
clear of my sulking, terror,
dry compulsion,
clear of the lot, where
the lot has been fairly seen.

The World in the Shadow of God

II.

We are crouching in the marsh,
the reeds tall and thick.
The water at our ankles licks
up our legs with its large
muddy tongue seeping
through our pants, what's left
of our clothing. No one sleeps.
The birds return with our breath
stilled, but clatter away
with the passing pillage, the shots
fired, the shouts raised.
The mud's air rots
in our mouth and noses.
Wiping our bellies in the stream,
the dark settles and grows.
Tonight we do not dream.

Burundi, 1965, 1969, 1972, 1988, 1993, 1994–2004.

23. Pontius Pilate

I.

A rabbi said to me
once, gravely—
too gravely—
"To do one's best
is not enough!"
But I say better,
still better than
to vaunt the rest.

I wear gloves, you see,
thick scarves,
dark trousers
tight at the ankle,
firm, buttoned boots,
cufflinks like locks,
silk cravats, tugged—yes,
I am well dressed,
And—now this is capital—
I am fully covered.

Who should ever wish
to see my tendons,
taut, crooked? Why,
it even aches to think of
such striated members,
furrowed by grasping,
embossed with veins,
bloated and exhausted,
by nature scarified.
Modesty forbids . . .
I close the curtains
when I bathe,

as no doubt
does the rabbi.

The nations,
mark me, the nations
know the garden's shame
as well as any
prophet has described
its honor lost.
Yet we have learned
(and I am but
a humble representative)
far finer weaves
than leaf and hide.
We have in some
small way redeemed
a measure for the eye.

The eye! The eye
is hope especially
if we must be failures,
waiting at last
to be exposed,
all of us and in the end,
and I also,
to skulk away
in lurid excess.
The fault is ineluctable.
But dash it, man,
why bugger in the daylight
when there is still
left night for
deep discretion?
I call it nothing less
than pity.

II.

You pray for the peace of Jerusalem,
as your David said. It seems, for him,
as it seems for you, that perhaps in time
the world can finally be untied.

But Jesus, Jesus, don't you know
that winter is warm and death is slow?
Thus, Jesus, why do you pray for peace
as if it contradicts the least

of God's instantaneities?
For the fullest draught of deity
lies in the shortest breath of life.
I prove this by my father's wife:

she leeched her sorrowed soul away
over hours and hours that were added to days,
and days that were added to years and years
of which the end could only near

the end of God's quick reach.
But endlessness for her was speech
in wild turmoil. It always is.
So, Jesus, only aim for His

most singular and pressing points,
scattered round the world's disjointed
spirit. Jesus, time's a thief.
Jesus, Jesus, God is brief.

24. Was Crucified

I.

The piano wouldn't play.
After being dragged onto a ship,
hoisted, pushed, dropped and roped,
the piano couldn't play one note
and many others balked and sipped
clumsily away
between the cracks.

As ordered, they thrust her aboard
at Boston's knotted port,
a great brown, smooth thing
in polished wood, with insides ringing
softly as the sweating cohorts
of dockers swung her toward
the darkened hold.

She couldn't play right,
after tossing through the damp
off Florida, edging into Nassau
where the rats fell to gnawing.
Near Matthew Town hammered
by a storm's raw fist all night,
the song bled out her ears.

Silent she was, in San Juan,
while all the others drank and thrashed.
They drew her to St. Kitts, mute,
settled in a torpor, emptied by the brute
humidity, past Dominica in flashing
rains, her will had utterly gone
even before the crest of Pelee showed.

Ephraim Radner

It was a wasted hulk they left
there at Fort-de France, shoved in a cart
shaken on the little road, the asses
slowly jerking up the incline's last
twist before the small house perched apart
from the world where she rested
finally on its porch facing the sea.

"Make the damned thing play!",
was all he could bark out
to the wretched figure who clutched his hat
on the step. He waited and he sat
above the island sea, pouting
until the keys were all laid
straight and true,

until the felts were cut,
dried, glued over the hammers' heads,
the new strings stretched and racked,
fastened tight, and boards re-tacked,
the warps straight, vices shed
like a skin when time has shut
its usefulness away.

His impatience flapped stronger
as the workman busied over the weeks.
He kicked him twice and spat.
"Make her play, you fattened
pig! Or would you rather Martinique
still putrify a little longer
before she hears my music?"

The World in the Shadow of God

II.

It was summertime.
God loves raccoons. Here by the road,
with dust and grime stuck to its feet,
its eyes flashes of light, froth flowed
from out its mouth, to greet

the cat. He bit her twice.
Inside the sour Queen-Anne's lace
the vice-grip of his jaws squeezed out
two ghastly screeches. Then he paced
away. Some time, just about

autumn, in the woods
a girl approached the cat beneath
some pines. It stood there, steaming, bright.
Then, as the girl leaned in, its teeth
and spittle grabbed her right

hand. So each fled,
with nothing said to anyone.
Later, in the red-walled room
where the priest had put his desk, she'd run
into his arms. The bloom

that filled her face
spurred on his hands inside her dress.
His heart was racing when she gasped,
then bit him hard, quite hard, though less
hard than the cat, the last

time round, but full of white,
a warm white child-spume. It was hell
for priests that winter. No snow came.
God buried His raccoon. The leaves fell
and in the woods, a light rain.

25. Died

They waited for the trees.
When the rains came, so did the leaves,
which billowed out like wet air from within,
wrapping the spaces and vacant land
with small, fragrant arms and hands.

They had lost children that year.
The winter had been dry, smearing
everything with dust, even inside.
But now a rabbit, small, black
would come out at dusk. He sat

in the new grass by the trees.
He wasn't really a child, was he.
But that was fine. It was fine even so.
He was shiny, soft, and he stood
like a tiny glimmer in the woods.

26. And Was

We are all curious.
The important words, I know, are always clear;
and how they shimmer even casually
to those far off—
may I never forget!
Yet I too wonder what it was
you wrote stooped in the dust
as she stood before you,
still with tangles in her hair and sweating
while they asked if she might die.

How we know of your mercy.
It drips from the prayers we keep turning,
copied, bound, hurled into the fire,
retrieved, remembered, recommended.
It was the figure of a woman, was it not?
The line of her back
like ash blown against a stone;
in raised regret,
the slipping contour of one arm held hesitant
at the soft pads of her fingers;
a single stroke tilts back her face
limned in mingled rose and gray.

She had another name—
not she whom conscience crept away from mocked—
another one, whose name before,
whispered in limpid syllables of an ancient tongue
fled and with her padded fingers
gently pressed upon the nations,
gently closed her quiet lids
on this year's quiet dews,

while they will ask again, confident, bright,
might she die this time please?
This one, whose quiet lines you kissed and dropped.
This one, whom you drew and we saw it not.
This one, whose name we never caught.

27. Buried

I.

They're after your suitcase
with its brushes and razors
caught in the traffic
of socks and blue shirts.
All bought many years ago

on a number of streets,
after several meetings,
with their cooled tumblers
lined beneath the windows,
unwound on an iced spool of earnest talk.

Well, we've peeked inside of it.
We've fingered its size,
its creaking hinges,
with its perfumes underneath and clothes.
We want to travel with the linen, chatter, beguile

each other and you.
We want a rueful
rub at your cuffs
and their cracked starch
wiped against the troubles and thought and sight

you bought and handled
through various stands
at night and in taut
mornings of little sun.
What you have touched we would touch in flight.

We touch your eye.
Where the hair lies
wild, we brush it.
We fold your stretching limbs.
With you, with the locks, we cast all to the piled sea,

to safety. Never
will they find or separate
flesh and faithful
wandering, drinking, drooping
carelessness—the treasure, the water, scattered.

Ephraim Radner

II.

We must believe that some things will never be.
We must hold them far from us,
stiffening our arms and clamping down their heads into the deep waters,
so that when the sun skims off the surface all is flat and clean
but for the floating weeds.

Rich and poor alike hope with the same eyes
dead set in the head,
close at the center but vague and frayed at their unsteady edges,
cooling, where sight dare not topple over and peer,
does not and cannot wish,

gropes back to the boat-rails with every reason in place.
Like the kelp, undisturbed,
no need to look up or about, they sway in tepid green suspension;
alike even in work and patience and dumb resolve,
preparing and prepared for thirst

along with a raft of solid provisions—something we always
carry just for safety.
Here are shrewd judgments, honed distinctions that comfort breeds upon.
To stay afloat is the whole brittle triumph of our ruse.
Such is knowledge we can trust.

28. He Descended

There is quite a collection at the top
of various sizes:
bags, bricks, a trunk
lopped of leaves
which dries in the sun.
There is always a sun which sticks up stiffly,

a sign waving down
at the small hopers
with their gathered luggage
bound with tapes
and twine ropes.
All of them would rather huddle higher,

swathed in light. Do they know
how they will linger,
once lifted, the same even more,
preserved from the lowlands
as things unchanged
by the absence of blame or of great depleting duty?

Few items rot
at such bone-dry heights.
Sisyphus, it's easily gotten
up there. Take courage.
For only once
in this business will it crash down.

29. To the Dead

I have only seen things
through the window.

There was the accident,
the shattered glass like summer ice.

I saw her slap his face next door
then draw the curtains of a drab color.

A child, thoughts elsewhere,
tripped and wept and had to raise herself,
for she was walking on the street alone.

When the clouds lift and the light is strong,
the ocean rises into view as if blown,
from where, I know.

I know they send us messengers from there
that set our teeth together on an edge,
that make pity droop and shield herself.
Messages rush in, come from another country.

My glass is hard enough.
It does not clatter like milk bottles at dawn.
It does not swing or chime.
My clarity is quiet in this home.

I have one opening, one space,
a draught that blows out from my chest.
She has no blinds, no glass, no heaviness.
When the ocean rises, none.
When the light is strong, only light;
when the other country passes through
with its words destined for the other side.

30. On

The sky had cleared.
Yet the man beside me pointed to the blue
bearing down on us
like a helmeted boar
who gleams, ignorant.
Quietly, he said
that such a storm would blow your ears off.

I took the turns more quickly.
We spun more quickly still,
as the pleasure of the sky,
in endless spasm,
seemed to reel, collapsing upwards.

The man beside me chattered,
now roused with breathless satisfaction.
He knew two girls struck dead
upon the hills,
fetching wood, bits of wood,
tied up in packets for their head.
And last year, did you hear?
the ten in town
who added to their sorrow
with the sky's availing reach?
He sniggered at the funeral
on which a bolt of lightning fell
scattering the ten new corpses on the field,
hymnals sprayed across the grass,
like the sky now come down,
faster than the car.

Ephraim Radner

Throwing herself at us
like family, yearned across
the distances,
she had come.

We reached the summit of the hill
just as she let sound
the bellows of her linings,
alive, spread through the hush
like blood butter.
The man beside me tingled visibly and smiled,
teeth and tiny holes alight.
And I, I flew,
down the other slope
intent to pass below
as she passed on above.

31. The Third Day

My dears—

On our second night out
we reached a ring where the sea was flat
like a smooth and rounded threshing-floor.
We waited for the moon

to rise and lay itself
across the black glass waters.
We stood together at the railing
and watched as they pushed out.

Their small boats circled
with the lamps swinging a feeble light,
less than the moon's, less than the ship's.
I took April to me.

We danced for half an hour.
I thought of you through the quiet music.
They were still circling when we stopped.
Their voices drifted to us,

calling, and the lamps squeaked.
When they had glided to the side,
I asked them what it was they were after,
so long out and so far.

A burly man in the shadows
told us a child had drowned years back,
in that spot, falling over the rails.
They always returned in season.

Ephraim Radner

After the boats were lashed,
the motors started and pushed us on.
We reach port by morning, I'm told.
I will send this then.

32. He Rose

With all the stones the angel rolled away,
he built a wall.
He rolled so many thousand.
Gathering them all,
he raised up four sides around an unknown
space, high, impregnable, distillate, clear,
enumerated through the passing years:

In the dark place lies a little garden,
sown with seeds of tiny, crystal dew.
And in the garden there is grass,
whose sap is hot and never hardens.
And in the grass there plays a child,
who looks straight ahead, as if she knew.
And in the child beats the heart
that trembles like the moon gone wild.
And in her heart there sighs a breath
of pleasure, taken, lost, unguarded.
And in the breath there flows an air,
seeping through the soil, bounding over death.
And in the air there hangs a star
that always spins, though never dwindles.
And in the star, light upon light,
that wraps around the close, still and far.
And in the light, a single cry.
The burdened angel staggers
in delight at it.

33. Again

When Mary weeps once more, she seems
much like the wall in front of me.
Against it leans the altar, and
above it a yellow window, fenced
in by a rail. It is her tears
I think of, where the wall is split.
Up near the glass the plaster sinks
and drips roll down. It cannot last,
I told them, or the wood will rot.
Instead, it's lack of funds or skill
to do the work. Not once, but five
times I was jerked around by men
who didn't show, or asked for fees
that outstripped reason. What is there
to do? The cracks grow larger, ripping
pieces whole onto the floor,
and scattering dust in circles. We keep
painting over. Though the yellow
window creaks, we sweep the faint
spray at its feet, and wait for worse,
if anything. Now these are Mary's
tears, this way of working wonders.
How we can pray most anywhere
today! But such is modern prayer.

34. He Ascended

If you look down on the plains,
this is what you see:
After the rains, the fields
sown, the beasts gathered,
herded, their breath revealed
in the mellow sun, blown
softly; words are sung;
sacrifices of yellow grain
and rich meat flung
on the fires; rising towns
are pitched, embraced by rivers
that water the earth, timeless;
women bloom, whom the race
of angels fall after;
sweat drips, and assumes
luxuriant flesh; stilled
air settles and rises
steamy, lilting, restful;
at night, fair lullabies.

But here, everything is clear;
the rivers are small, you hear
the water's cold shiver;
the shadows roll quickly
down; the trees gather
in each lone crack;
few people roam;
only a marvelous wind.

35. Into Heaven

She wrapped the box in music sheets.
Inside, she said, she had laid her heart
as a prize. It was carefully done from the start,
each page pulled tight, the corners neatly

folded, the glue applied. But somewhere
the box was lost, delayed, put aside.
It finally came, but he had died.
Everything was placed upstairs

in the attic: letters, cards, the box too.
When his daughter found it years after,
she sought to open it, and in the bathroom
to steam the sheets that water and glue

had merged into one. Tugging with tongs
and tweezers, scraping a little, she lifted
each page, peeling back the gift's
covering: two weeks of a long

excavation. There were four layers.
She could make out the names of a few
pieces: *Moment Musical*, *Salut
d'Amour*— awkward and maudlin prayers

of a lost affection. But only the last
had notes. She dried and then she pressed it:
Kreisleriana— difficult, but less
than some, though she began it too fast.

The World in the Shadow of God

Over several days, one hand at a time—
it was only one page, and she would buy
the rest—she patiently worked, and tried
to make it perfect, line by line.

"This must be my father," she thought,
as her hands moved, easy and firm,
and her mind opened, and everything she learned
flowed. She could not remember him as she ought.

This she had always felt, groping
for signs, in pictures, in what was told her.
Now, for a moment, she knew. And the old
box, stripped bare, she left unopened.

36. And Is Seated

The Tartars pass on quietly outside.
With the wind they pull along loose newspapers.
Now a man stops at the window
and mouths some words to me.

"Can we go . . . ?", he shouts perhaps.
His legs are wrapped in paper,
his calves whipped by the gusts.

He motions with enthusiasm.
"Carry on!", I think he yells.
I rather think he tells me this,
before he flies away
with his newsprint and his empty bags unfurled.

My drink remains unusually warm
and its breath still rises.
Good God, and daylight too,
and daylight too goes running past.

37. At

It happens, when the massive gate is opened,
that you can walk in, with the city at
your feet. It's rare. But otherwise, there's no
way in or out. A man will come, whose hat
is gold, whose robes are red; he runs, his patter
naked-sounding on the street's bare stones.
He has a key, and gathered throngs are glad
to see him fit it in the lock's great hole.
With all his strength he turns it. And the crowd
stares at his work. A shot is heard, a crack
breaking the air—ock is sprung! The people
wait, transfixed. They stand there in their thousands—
soldiers, workmen, farmers with strong backs.
Yet no one pushes at the door or speaks.

38. The Right Hand of the Father

Gordon loved the fishes
and Maisie loved the mice.
She loved their fur and let it settle
up against her fingers, thrice
beloved, pet at morning,
afternoon and evening,
the last before she slept, shoved
against the wall and a pillow
and deep slumber caressing.

She loved the leaves.
While Gordon let the fishes die
in the sink, she rubbed their veins
against the emptied butterflies
whom the wind swept up
in autumn piles, with moths
the fluff of the world's room,
this room where she ran and played,
lay and slept, cheek against earth.

Gordon cleaned the bowls
while Maisie pet and cooed.
Their golden scales went dull and rolled
with the spin of the drain.
They disappeared, and next the tears
as Gordon wept their loss,
so unexpected, clean, and fearless.
"I am brave too," he said.
"I will live to see another fish."

The World in the Shadow of God

The mouse was given freedom.
Three times a day it ran
about the room of pastel walls,
then up the sleeves of her brand-
new coat, autumn wool,
scarlet dye, a girl's dream.
The creature rested there, grew
very cold. Discovered days later
by her poking arm, it fell as she dressed.

39. He Will Come Again

I.

Like as the hart
rushing through brush and clearing,
amid trees and startled light,
peering, panting,

every pagan
looks behind himself,
an Actaeon pursued. His legs
churn, he finds

no rest as he breaks
the rich stew of the earth
and makes the twigs shatter,
renewing the chase

each day, as desire hounds
and drives, faster and faster,
pounding deeper and deeper,
always from behind,

with her dogs. Every pagan,
every forest run through,
trampled, everything played
from behind, stunned

like deer, desperate
for distance. But when deer become men!
Look here, friend! Ahead,
the gods reverse themselves!

The World in the Shadow of God

II.

The hippopotamus knows better than I.
He knows the thinking of the fly.
He sinks into the mud and lies
with its soft and motherly protection,

while all the bites and the buzzes break
above, the air settling, the snakes
resting, horror hidden and making
only small noises at the edge of the grass.

"Stay away!", he says wisely. Stay away and let
the world's crashing be gently set
within the leaves of God's book that rests,
pages and chapters, upon His long shelves.

When the river boils and time
comes to its hiccough and all the signs
in the sky glare and comets are flying,
then his skin shall peel and he will pray.

40. To Judge

I.

Hattie's is out of business.
The drinks are finished,
the sign on the door.
I don't go there anymore.

They want to sell for half a million,
but who's willing?
It's been months and ages.
I figure there's no way.

You can look in the windows and see
the tables, the green
chairs, the napkins all new
as if waiting to be used

to wipe lips that are wet
with talking, speckled
with beer; all of it wasted
over the years. It's something you face

as you walk down the street
and stare at the steep
pile of money and words
you spent over the years, turned

over to people gone bust.
What was it?
Let us wipe our mouths:
napkins are for now.

The World in the Shadow of God

II.

When Parente's truck comes by,
clanging its bell
we all come out of our homes with knives
set for sharpening.
In back is the pile of his store:
five blades for food,
for separating joints and bones
for slicing away
the layers of fat, flesh to cubes,
for peeling and the hard chopping;

four instruments to cut the trees:
an axe and hatchet,
long sheers and small clippers;

three tools to break the earth,
to dig, to hack,
to drag as you plough;

two swift scissors,
a large one for the man's clothes,
a small one for the child's—
cziizz, they go, ground sharp.

And one tiny scalpel,
gleaming and very, very smart,
to cut into the heart.

Ding, ding, ding!
his bells ring out.
He is an old man now,
but he knows many things.

Ephraim Radner

III.

The house is near the corner of the street.
On either side are open lots, kept trimmed.
The bungalows down the block, when the summer heat
comes, smell like the old fruit the wind

has blown from the trees to the sidewalks. Inside the house
they are sitting at a table, talking. Then one
of them stands up. He waves his hand, aroused
by something said. Someone is dying, not young,

but not old. She is in a room, far from the kitchen
where the chairs are ranged, and the talk goes on, and the light
just at this hour marks every line. A decision
will be made. But first the horror and the fight

against guilt and losing will be waged in this place.
Everything in its place, God putting a last
point to it, the light fixing it, the people, the spaces,
the tears, and the time just so, at last.

IV.

In a corner of the garden
flattened up against the green,
a dead rabbit lies,
its flesh already hardened,
its wounds wrapped in a sheen
of iridescent flies
bright blue and copper.

Through the top of its small head
its inner form had run
through an open wound,
whose faded colors bled
and blanched within the sun.
The neighbor's cat had chewed him,
as had the small white worms,

as will the blackbirds, turning
to the squirrels, who wonder,
dancing and yelling: where
the corpse is, there must surely
come the ravens, plundering,
and wisdom, unclothed to the stares
of her children and their friends!

Send here the children of the wise!
They are raised in the schools of the Emperor.
They grow into his courts,
retainers, bowing and rising,
nurses, supple and tender,
builders of temples and ports,
soldiers in their coats,

blue and copper, their throats
buttoned, boots gleaming.
Their bridges span the web
of His canals, His boats
fly colored banners, streaming,
maidens make His bed,
peasants cut His beard,

oxen rear His calves,
orchards bear His fruit,
women weave His clothes
while His scholars etch their paths
to knowledge, the singers and their flutes
trill, the gardeners mow,
sorrow fades into the grass.

At last I go to the King!
Take me quickly where
the language of the beasts
is the song of the wise singing.
I too shall bow down there
in the garden corner's peace,
dissolving in its hum.

(Luke 7:35; 17:37)

41. The Living

We saw an angel too.
It had a vile tail of rough and point,
tiny mushroom ears, a blue tongue,
something curious in its tough, dark eyes

that glowered ever so
over the wet deck, twitching and aflame . . . . Oh,
it's too much, when we're stowed away at night
to insist that God might love the peeping rats

as much as a hustling man.
Yes. It was *his* angel, we admit; not ours.
And when we fancy their flesh, and eat at its ends
we but submit to the blood that sends shivers in the spirits' shoes.

They attract the lust of the gods.
They always have; and we long for the way their hands
curve about the ropes and nodding spars
of the ship, as they'd fan round heaven's large hips.

They are beloved, apt,
guilelessly agile creatures—hence their stupidity.
But we listened, rapt, as rescue was proffered through the wind
and the men filed sullenly back with their skins drenched.

What a little God can do!
spread over the ocean, running to the land,
smoothed over with a man's kisses and attentions.
We were the first in the water, the first on the sand, the last missed.

(Saint Paul preaches to the ever-resentful rats—Acts 27)

42. And the Dead

When my daughter reached the age of one,
the Spring came well. I thank
my God for changing her into the shells
that line the shore, and rustle
white and gold and pink
before the roar.

My daughter grew to ten years old.
The Fall crept up on her.
I thank the Lord He held her face and leapt
high in the trees, while casting
her into their branches
as they ran the breeze.

When she was twenty-five, my daughter glistened
with the Winter of that
year. O God be praised, you deigned to splinter,
splay, and still her heart
as wood that comes of age,
and in the snow is laid.

The years of wisdom are these Summer hours.
Have we all not been blessed
by them? O blessed God, that she has reached
this time; be blessed again.
Now she is heat and dryness both.
This I confess.

43. I Believe In

Give me your face
and let me see
beneath the rain and windowsill
if it is still the same, still cherishes
my hunger and my greed.

Give my your cheeks
blown out wide
like a sheet before the rain,
to strain my thumbs against and greet
their rippling sides.

Your sockets, will they hold me?
The walls that run along
your skull, will they support
the force of my fingers, the mulling fondness
they bring on?

Your chin like a chair,
may I sit in it?
Will it swing and sway this rainy day,
under the weight I fling inside,
if only for a minute?

You have known me and you love me.
Then why has the land
become so soggy, creased, and pasty,
your bones chased up the trees, your flesh
swallowing my hands?

44. The Holy Spirit

I.

This is what I wish for:
clean socks, a ticket for the train,
and when it is over,
under the boughs, on a table cloth,
a basket of fruit.

In it are my people,
truly arranged
in color and in health,
in size and heaviness,
the fragile on the top,
safe for one long afternoon.

Not in a bag,
not in running,
not dropped or crushed
as the flat and heated pavement
crushes things.
How I would wish it otherwise.

But not to us, O Lord.
Not to us, nor to me.
I have soles on my feet,
but cannot walk this hot cement.
Heart have I,
yet cannot pound it out.
Throat have I,
yet will not cry.
Those I protected are like me,
their hands flat against my own,
drawn in safety and a circle.

The World in the Shadow of God

Not to us but to you,
whose breath ripens limbs
from green to scarlet skin,
swelling to the dropping;
whose sun drips sugar through our pores
until the branches throb;
placed close to the cut,
whose lips and teeth give suck
and draw our whispers out,
both small and great.

Not I, but you have done with wishing,
now and ever.
Not I but you, clothed and ready,
travel knowingly, lightly, completely.

II.

St. Philip was flying through the sky,
the wind blowing where it will.
He looked down and saw the plain,
the acacia trees dotting the high
grass, the dark swathes of forest
swelling out from the edge. He saw
the animals, the night beasts, even their eyes.
There were monkeys, perhaps people at the lakeshores.
But he wanted to preach to them all, all of them
his daughters. "Hey you!", he cried; "you there
below!" The wind was blowing as he flew by.
The animals looked up, drank it in, and crawled on.

The World in the Shadow of God

III.

The Father is dry,
the Son is moist
with blood as he is hoisted,
so says the fool, to die.

The Father squeezes
out each drop
from the Son's brow, from his hot
lips, as they mumble peace,

as he cries,
as he lives
with the beasts, and gives
life's liquor and its rising.

"But the blood's not mine!"
the Son pleads.
"Not mine at all. It bleeds
from all the Father's time

and more besides!
What's mine is His
first, and only from this
does water from my side

flow down."
The one dry thing
is the world's brittle being,
which God's Floods will drown.

Ephraim Radner

For God is moist
all over, drunk
with waters He has flung
through heaven's rasping noise.

He carouses and oozes
in spaces and cracks,
His green River tracking
the rocks and rendering them smooth.

45. The Holy

Most old boats have windows
that never open. And should they,
with the weather ringing in their faces?
This one had a string of them,
like a row of black buttons, hem to collar,
on a floating fat man's tunic,
lapsed on its side.
The sun's slide against their sheen
left the gleaming eyelets dark and close.
The sky at three o'clock is colorless
but for the bleached and reeling clouds.

We passed around the ship
three times, fast and slow.
We tapped at the windows,
each one a dull rap
giving nothing but a gull's reflection
in return as they flew by uncivilly,
the land distant and blue,
just as the sea is on other days.
We peered in through the sightless holes,
but there was only darkness folded in bundles
and tossed into corners the sun ignored.

When we boarded her, the waves had risen,
just shaving the deck with their white edges.
We yelled into the deepening light,
into the gusts and swells,
shaking the padlocked doors and unrusted bolts
someone had oiled for the storm.
An idea formed in the silence among us.

Ephraim Radner

Over the side, we left in haste and spray.
We could have towed her in that day
but for the wind.
She crashed down suddenly at four,
the air restored to her pallor.
We flew before her blush, running all the way.
I know we could have towed her on another day.
We would have surely done so.

46. Catholic

I.

The Lord went to a lonely place to pray.
He walked and whistled to his dog, a loud
bright sound. The dog ran up to him and bowed
his head, his mouth grinning and dripping away.

They stepped among the stones. The evening light
revealed a swarm of desert flies had flown
above from Egypt, as the cool had grown
and brought his floating whistle to their flight.

They flocked to him, as did the locusts, working
with their mouths, who seemed to chew the air
around them. Then came the jackals, the bears
crawling behind from rocks where they were lurking,

The birds above gathered into knots
of feathers, as they rode the breezes down
to where the Lord had stopped, the ground
teeming with beasts and even swine, whose hot

and filthy keeper had run off. The howl
they made—for all were howling—reached the sky,
where evening darkened with deep wings. A sigh
hung over the earth. There, creeping things, and fowl,

and furred things and scaled, bright beings ran,
while the Lord stood still and prayed. With every word
he passed out scraps—to each, unhurried—
bits that he had brought. He first began

by tossing to the dog, and one by one,
he prayed and fed the others: peelings scraped
from gourds, in thin, long, withered, yellow strips;
the muddied pulp of cold beans dug out from

the bottom of a pot the night before;
small lumps of beaten grains, ground in a paste.
All these he cast about him, as he praised
our God. The night seized and lifted up the roaring

swell they made, warm and alive. The beasts
each gave their thanks, each bowed, each laid a kiss
upon his feet and thanked our God. As if
into the moon's loose, melting light of peace,

he sent them out, each praising God, each blessing
God. He sent them out to do their task,
to grow, to overcome the nations, fast
and marvelous, crying, subduing, pressing.

II.

The hawk could see
beneath the stone's bare weight
a gathering of mice
and so he ate,

the sound of which
did nothing to appall
the other beasts, and nature
least of all.

Said the aphid to the ant,
"Your hole is dry and deep
just as my leaf is wide.
But I can seek

no other refuge
for my family or my fear than this
wet space flooded
by all, by bliss,

by avid light,
by anger and by accident;
no other place to loiter
on events,

their backs and legs
as fragile as your own.
With a pulley I hoist you up.
You will be shown

the stones and rodents,
the crooked arc of wings
as they pass by in violence,
the words they sing.

We will raise them all in turn,
you and I, with levers,
to glory in the spectacle on high
until the birds retrieve us."

47. Church

I.

I have known elephants,
their noses so long that even they
are hung in embarrassment.
They squirm and writhe,
a fated prospect for their own astounded eyes.

I was married to an elephant.
I could not sleep for fear
of having love squeezed from my ribs.
I wrestled with her shame,
her hapless, independent body and her bane.

Tell me your secrets,
I whispered coyly,
thinking, her ears have welcomed mine before.
When she sat silently I tried
to get mine back and with a twisted branch I pried.

But grass is thick and rooted
past her lobes, a plain that lengthens
from the East into the Western open holes;
so far has she removed my muttered smiles
and planted stubble in their place. It goes for miles.

My only rest is in her head,
along the scaly furrows, between her eyes,
as a friend in concert with astonishment,
slowly covered, where she lives, by the water and the earth,
at last by her skin, at one with her enormous girth.

Ephraim Radner

II.

It is a grim voice, very grim,
if small, without a bottom to it.
She sounds from underneath a stone
which every day I circle around,
smooth and mottled brown
like an old man's head—
a tiny piece of rock that covers
all the dark world's uttered dirt
deep sown in its belly.

What does the small voice say?
That soil is there, compressed,
that all the greens and browns,
the earth's shades cast about,
that all the ancient grass,
the rotten woods, the gaseous fumes,
the sod and all her worms arrayed
in restless glory—
that they lie there,
lie there and speak,
rumble at my feet and blare.

O fair one! Snatch me
far from all such greens,
rampant and reaching,
from all greens and browns,
from claylike tints
that stink and stick on
to my clothes, my sides,
save me clear from such an earth
and all her soiled smile.

III.

Outside the Church, dancing;
outside, the fury of loveliness
cast about the tails of trees.
Outside the Church, singing;
outside, the winds whisked
into cities and clouds bartering
colors, always in joyful profit.
Outside the Church, everything held high,
the moisture runs wild,
the droplets make oceans,
in whose blue souls swim.

Inside, we enter the hollows
of substance where one thing follows
the next, I know not why.
Inside, only stones that call us
to stand here or there,
spaces often spare, none swallowed,
objects, one after another.
Inside, light only inches forward
from the edges. The Fall is
like Winter and Summer, the Spring
weighty. Nothing can gall us
in any moment; all is itself.
Grays and white, light inches
forward. My toes pulse. Malice
has ceased weeping. Inside, the cracks
slowly fill, even the smallest.

Extra ecclesiam nulla salus,
but for what's already mentioned.

IV.

Father Confessor always heard
the secrets of the people's pickled hearts.
His hut lay on the nearer part
of the great hill of stones and dirt
that rises from the sea,

yellow in Summer, black with the ice,
empty green at Spring and Fall.
One year, the fishes died. Then all
the people, dragging carts with sighs
and walking glumly, left.

The old man waited through the months,
fingering the tiny rocks outside his door.
At dusk he'd climb the hill. The wind tore
in from far away, like drums.
He strained to hear. It seemed

he caught some words of deep remorse,
distant, their small ends flying in the gusts
just as his hair flew back with dust.
At last the birds blew in, the force
of their descent like heat.

Reeling around, each one cried out,
"I've sinned! I've sinned! I've sinned!". The old man fell
onto his knees. He ached to tell
his Lord, in tears, shouting with thanks, "Let them say more!"

V.

The Cardinal waves his hand goodbye;
the merchant turns aside and sighs.
Nunc dimittis,
it is finished,
Babylon the great now cries.

Babylon must watch and cry,
the Cardinal is passing by.
Magnificat,
the wife of Lot,
her husband's tears already dried.

Her husband's tears have long since dried,
the merchant's chests are all untied.
Vox clamantis,
the church in Pontus,
and all of Asia too has died.

All of Asia's wasted pride,
all Europe's sales unsatisfied.
Quid est veritas?
In the Americas
bow down, the Cardinal passes by.

The Cardinal is passing by;
the nations of the world ask why.
Noli me tangere,
The Church is on parade
with all her banners flying high.

48. The Communion

I.

On His third drink,
God leaned back,
waved over the city.
"You know, I think
I like these damned poor folk
and all their giddy
ways."

He gasped as He grabbed
His neighbor's stool.
"I like their open roofs,
the wind that sags
in and out of broken panes.
I like their soothing porches.

When it's hot,
they lie out like dogs;
when the dog dish freezes,
they pile the rot
of broken chairs and boxes where
they and the fleas
once dozed.

I like their screen
doors, that hang
as wet, thin slices peeled
from a loaf of green
bread. I like the mud around
their windows, congealed
with dinners

which loom up the way
an iceberg floats.
I like their quickness. Who
can ever say
how quick they are? When all is lost,
the whole crew
is out,

they're on the street,
with cans and bags,
pink baby dresses
trail sweetly
in the gutter. I like their colors
and the dance lessons
they share."

He leaned back in,
holding his neighbor's
shoulder. "Bless their tribe.
The thing that I can
always count on poor folk for,
is keeping my eyes
on them."

II.

Some time after
he had died,
Augustine went to Ostia.
It was a way to grasp
again the goodbyes
and their places before he forgot their cost.

Where is my son?
Where is my mother?
And the one woman whose name I have lost?
His thoughts were running
together with others.
Did his father wear a cross?

It was growing season.
The wheat was cascading
down the hills to the sea like oil
flowing easily
and glistening in the fading
sun along the sloping soil.

"This is like Africa!"
he remembered, though he wondered
if Asia too had such glowing fields.
Wandering about, laughing
and stroking the tender
stalks, even peeling

back their skin—
it was like the woman's hair,
their fingers and faces entwined, as God spoke:
"It is time to begin
the planting," whereupon
Augustine replied, still stroking

the wheat, "Goodbye!"
He watched his limbs
growing green at their roots, harden and leaf,
his hair shine,
gathered into thin
heads of grain like a wreath.

Her name was Daphne,
he thought as he changed.
"And an enemy shall sow among you . . ."
God's voice, laughing,
trailed away.
"I shall wait", Augustine mumbled.

III.

I've never heard the raven's call
nor shared with him a cigarette.
We've never had an earnest talk
while sitting on a park banquette.

He's never asked me to his home,
nor spoken of his many sons.
He's never cursed his uncle's hands
nor mentioned friends he's shunned.

We once have had a drink or two
though it was somewhat on the fly:
he above and I below,
as the rain came sweeping by.

49. Of Saints

Here is a beetle,
its trace in white scar-tissue.
Had I tweezers of the sort,
we could all see.
The beetle, bright and small,
hatched within my thigh,
its tongue and heel and flashing prongs
that scoop itself a home
down beside my bone.

Have you a beetle too?
As black as your tongue and slippers?
I'm sure you do,
although I never knew my own
until its tiny feet appeared
across my skin and ran for cover
further in, where my blood is sullen,
less excitable, less gay.

Since then it has engineered
galleries of unwound space,
long catacombs to track beside my veins and vessels.
It has dug on and wandered,
painting as it goes the walls
behind which capillaries flow
quiet and earnest.
It daubs each smoked-up corner brown and ochre,
with hunters and bison tied at the feet
by dancers with their spears.
They have been leaping now for years.

Ephraim Radner

My beetle draws a shaft inside
as well as any god can fashion
thunderbolts without.
This is a warning to all fashioners,
of bone or wood or words.
When I drag my fingertips
along the roof of all these grooves,
the tunnels underneath begin to echo,
the streaks along my arms and back,
my stomach lined like my legs,
they rumble louder as the passages unfold,
the whole sea caught in a cave.

I do not shiver then,
but when my beetle thunders back.

50. The Forgiveness

I like to gaze through the curtain
in the late afternoon,
watching the light empty the street
of all but flayed form.

That day it was five and I saw
God arrive at the stoop.
He waited, then looked around, nervously,
saying something in silence,

rehearsing a speech or uttering
a word obsessively.
Then, climbing, he reached the top step.
He turned, as if looking at me.

Someone opened the latch.
God had a cap,
groped for it, took it off,
then stared at whoever stood there.

They talked a moment. Then God
walked in.
The phone rang, and so I never saw
him leave. But on the sidewalk

next morning, there was the cap,
perhaps still lying
out from the evening before. Again,
I sat by the curtain to watch.

51. Of Sins

I.

They met at the bottom of the hill
in a space between the trees.
The grass there was dried from the month's heat,
breaking between their feet.

So they faced each other. He said
quietly, grimly, "why
have you done this to me?". The other replied,
"you know." Indeed they knew

everything. They knew the past;
they knew what would come; and the insides
of things they knew. They were like the gods,
though like mortals falling.

There was no rain that year.
The brush was ground down
into a fine dust, caught up
in the air, like a great sail.

The World in the Shadow of God

II.

If we burn the house,
it makes no difference who is in it.
The fire is what counts.
Ten, thirty, fifty young men, it's
all the same—
the names, or whatever the race.
What counts are the flames,
the smoke, the cries, after the chase,
the parents at home,
the friends on the road, the long wailing
that plants its groan
in the ground and shoots up sailing
into the sky.
It is the fire that counts,
that runs through the fields,
that flies and flies
up the mountain sides, reeling
by the streams
and across the paths, out of my heart,
burning the seams of the world's rattling parts
over which Lucifer is king.
This day a nation of torches, bright
and wicked sings
of a new light.

Burundi, 1993—"Plus jamais ça"

III.

They are digging up the road in town.
Underneath are long canals
of smooth, green waters, without sound,
but teeming quietly in their foul

depths. Outside, above, there is a winding
down. People are wasting. When they sleep,
they turn from each other, their hand finding
a wall, or holding to their cheek the sheets.

They are slipping away, turning back to the dust
that covers everything, their smiles wan,
fingers and hair translucent, as if just
appearing, a mist as the dawn

breaks. Even now the waters are seeping
in, under the roads, welling up beneath houses,
small creatures, invisible to light, leaping
in the wet darkness, uncovered, and aroused.

Gonaives, Haiti

52. The Resurrection

I.

There is inside my mouth a stone.
A small hand placed it there,
alone, awash,
fair.

Stones do not grow flesh with time
freeing them. They give out
no sighs, nor grope
about

the soil in search of wriggling loves.
My child's stone will grow
in weight. Above,
below,

the rest of livingness and world
may flourish. But her rock
becomes the pearl
that mocks

all animate design. Just gifts
of brute, simple might—
their children lift
the light.

Ephraim Radner

II.

A few of them crept out of the rocks.
It was after a very long season, it seemed.

"Nothing is left" says the rat.
"I have nibbled for months,
licked the ceilings of the caves,
wiped the corners and the edges;
even the rims of things that lie deep.
Everything is clean, and I am fat."

The cockroach wobbles slowly through the cracks.
"I have populated the world!", he bleats.
"I am Abraham to the caverns under the earth.
My families have blessed the life of obscurity
with music and with song.
But we are too slow now for carnivals."

"As for me, there are only bones left," says the crab.
"They lie about, meatless, like stones."
He pulsates in his own shell,
pink, moist, vibrant.
"All flesh is mine!", he cries.
"But I am alone."

"No more eating," they all agree, "no more.
We are all tired of eating."

53. Of the Body

Sponges are cleaned incessantly.
When they were young, they seemed
free, waving in the tides,
riding the swirling currents.
Now, at their end, their work
done, spent, filled
with dirt, they will be wrung,
boiled, steamed, flung out.
They have wiped the soiled world.
Now is the right time for
wiping the world. How else
make up what is lacking in the vile
suffering that covers the back
of faith, hope, and love?

54. And

There are men,
after whom the women hobble,
who have no hair on their bodies.
I cannot blame them.
Did they ask the sun to blink
the morning of their birth?
Were they listening
that evening they slept soundly
with a frog's eye underneath the pillow?
But, oh what sorrow,
the day the final strand was plucked!

55. The Life

"I am still here."
This is the quickest way for me
to balance on my knee the moon,
its clanging light and brackets,
as I remember that, of course,
you are dead.
Tonight I clasp my knees in bed.
I pile on them the day,
the train I took that you had taken;
the city where you lived, that now
in one short year, has blossomed,
clearer, taller, surer of itself;
the restaurant where we ate,
the food is better now,
the smiles as I left more true.
The house that you had visited with me
has only me this evening.
And the day has hooks.
I hesitate to see what they have caught,
content with the pulling,
the jerking at their end
that slap against the sides.

I wish I had wires
to hold this contraption together,
to keep it from swaying too far,
from scraping the walls,
clanging like the moon
and only the moon can do.
I wish I had wire,
an eye for architecture,
and a name for all the noise my legs are bearing.

Ephraim Radner

I am still here.
My head is ringing,
searching for something
more imaginative.
And won't you need imagination more than I
where you have gone?
So here is mine in testament,
just as you are passing on to me
the bulk of your peculiar store.
What a land our parents moved to,
where anyone, even a brother and a sister,
can become rich!

56. Everlasting

I.

Hippos carry a heavy weight;
hence they are not happy-hearted
but are filled with hate.
Their jaws snap boats in parts,
while bodies quickly disappear.
So do their friends.
The buffalo have testicles that rear up,
whose resentment reaches the world's ends.
They will gore the Gentiles
out of rage at their own stolid loneliness.
The egrets follow their pounding, in file,
snatching the crickets
from the stomping, tantrumed feet,
cracking the shelled bodies, flinging them
lightly, neatly,
as the long river watches and sings
of another time, a peaceable time,
a hidden time.

II.

God bless the birds.
They have not heard or listened
as we have muttered and argued,
fastened to the stone.

They rise and fall,
calling to God alone.
Only the clouds nod
as He takes them to the far

side of the moon,
where they wait unknown.
They will fly up in a flock
when the air covers everything,

when the stars grow trees.
See! They swirl about,
shouting to the winter morning,
a knot untangling in the sky!

III.

The gardener had this dream. It was
the seventh hour and the sun
seemed hard. So entering in a flowerless
grove, he lay down in the shade

against a fallen log. Now time
had rotted out this tree and as
he slept, the soggy wood gave way.
He sees his head fall back into

the softened chips, and now his hair
soaks up their gritty moisture. Like
small bugs, the bark begins to shift.
It crawls across his mouth and pokes

into his nose, a deep red dirt
that marches through his head. His eyes,
in sleep, are covered by the rotted
core, and as he lies, the forest

seems to crumble on him—all
the wood becoming soil at his
ears, and teeming with small insects.
Someone whispers in the darkness

"Paradise," yet he can neither
see nor move to answer. Though
he tries to stand, he now is joined,
hands and feet, one with the growing

mound. "Paradise," the dust
is saying. "Paradise," the shining
termites sing, just as they reach
his skin. A worm is winding to

his heart, so slowly. Then, it breaks
the wall, at last, and light seeps out.
The gardener was awake. He stumbled
up. "I'm done with sleeping."

57. Amen

I.

Three pieces of meat
cut from the bone
end their bleeding.
They shall go home.

They shall depart from their place.
They shall leave the old town,
the shuttered shops and faces
turned with eyes cast down.

They shall find the path
to the side of the stream,
that crosses back,
that climbs up, green

as the hill, hugging the edge
of the oaks, blurred in the dark.
On the other side, hedges
run like raised scars.

They shall move through the grass
moist at dusk.
They shall find at last
the beasts, rustling,

stretching, resplendent with sweat,
with earth, sticky, steaming,
their bristling hides wet
like the grass, and almost gleaming.

Ephraim Radner

As they sigh,
there is a deep rumbling.
They lift their eyes
at the coming.

The meat of the Father,
the meat of the Son,
the meat of the Spirit
long since begun.

They shall go home now.
Flesh rejoices and howls.

II.

I am the buyer and seller.
They that go down to the sea in ships,
that do business in great waters,
they have seen my face
stamped on the sides of crates
about to be loaded.
Today or tomorrow we will go,
they say, into such a city;
continue for a year;
buy and sell and get our gain.
But I shall reap the profits.

I will rain them on the surface of the waves
like dry manure:
it is mixed and spread and pressed on down
to be a bed for trees,
for cedar and for cypresses.
Those that hew it
convey the same by sea on floats.
Those that drag the stones away
are given tools
for cutting out my likeness.
My features stir the levy on its way,
they mold the rising shapes
built on the hilltops.

Whose is this image on the coin,
propped in each worker's mouth?
Whose superscription?
You rub your fingers on my visage,
for whom the kings of all the earth
take custom and a tribute.

Ephraim Radner

Go to the sea and cast your hook
and you will find the same.
Should you toss it in for luck again,
remember that the slippery box
remains my own,
the tearful alabaster jar,
the poor with unwashed heads,
who never wander far,
filled with Satan and with spite.
The wages that I offer them are barely right,
I know.
But just, beyond all measure.

I sell such justice by the gates,
I gather and disburse.
The peoples come, they mass,
they trade and tax,
the sailors and the mates,
the builders and their slaves,
they stand far off and cry,
"What city is like unto this great city?"

And I ask you,
What do you think?
If I buy her, as I may,
you too may buy her back again,
with all your savings spent.
From whom then will you borrow?
Who then will come to lend?
I am the great Amen.

Bibliography

Aristotle. *Poetics*. In *Classical Literary Criticism*, translated by Penelope Murray and T. S. Dorsch. Harmondsworth: Penguin, 1965.
Augustine. *City of God and Christian Doctrine*. Nicene and Post-Nicene Fathers. First Series, Vol. 2. Peabody, MA: Hendrickson, 1994.
———. *Expositions of the Psalms. 1–32*. Edited by John E. Rotelle et al. Hyde Park, NY: New City, 2003
Bacon, Francis. *The Advancement of Learning*. Edited by William A. Wright. Oxford: Clarendon, 1885.
Barth, Karl. "No! Answer to Emil Brunner." In *Karl Barth: Theologian of Freedom*, edited by Clifford Green, 151–67. Minneapolis: Fortress, 1991.
———. *Protestant Theology in the Nineteenth Century: Its Background and History*. Grand Rapids: Eerdmans, 2002.
Bate, Jonathan. *The Song of the Earth*. Cambridge: Harvard University Press, 2000.
Blake, William. *The Complete Poetry and Prose of William Blake*. Edited by David Erdman and Harold Bloom. Berkeley: University of California Press, 1982.
Bly, Robert. *News of the Universe: Poems of Twofold Consciousness*. San Francisco: Sierra Club, 1980.
Boileau-Despréaux, Nicholas. *L'Art Poétique*. Edited by Guy Riegert. Paris: Larousse, 1972.
Bonaventure. *The Soul's Journey into God; The Tree of Life; The Life of St. Francis*. Translated by Ewert Cousins. New York: Paulist, 1978.
Bouillard, Henri. *Connaissance de Dieu*. Paris: Aubier-Montaigne, 1967.
Buckley, Michael J. S. *At the Origins of Modern Atheism*. New Haven: Yale University Press, 1987.
Burnet, Thomas, *The Sacred Theory of the Earth*. London: Centaur, 1965.
Clark, Donald Lemen. *Rhetoric and Poetry in the Renaissance: A Study of Rhetorical Terms in English Renaissance Literary Criticism*. New York: Russell & Russell, 1963.
Clarke, Adam. *The Holy Bible, Containing the Old and New Testaments. With Commentary and Critical Notes*. New York: Lane & Sandford, 1843.
Coleridge, Samuel Taylor. *Opus Maximum*. Edited by Thomas McFarland, with the assistance of Nicholas Halmi. Princeton: Princeton University Press, 2002.
Drummond, William. *William Drummond of Hawthornden: Poems and Prose*. Edited by Robert H. MacDonald. Edinburgh: Scottish Academic, 1976.
Foltz, Bruce V. *Inhabiting the Earth: Heidegger, Environmental Ethics, and the Metaphysics of Nature*. Atlantic Heights, NJ: Humanities, 1995.
Glacken, Clarence J. *Traces on the Rhodian Shore*. Berkeley: University of California Press, 1967.

Gosse, Philip Henry. *The Romance of Natural History*. Boston: Gould and Lincoln, 1862.
———. *A Year at the Shore*. London: Strahan, 1865
Gregory Nazianzen. *Select Orations*. Nicene and Post-Nicene Fathers. Second Series. Vol. 7. Peabody, MA: Hendrickson, 1994.
Haskins, Caryl Parker. *Of Ants and Men*. New York: Prentice-Hall, 1939.
Hauerwas, Stanley. *With the Grain of the Universe: The Church's Witness and Natural Theology*. Grand Rapids: Brazos, 2001.
Hobbes, Thomas. *Leviathan*. Edited by C. B. Macpherson. London: Penguin, 1968.
Horace. *On the Art of Poetry*. In *Classical Literary Criticism*, translated by T. S. Dorsch. Harmondsworth: Penguin, 1965.
Hume, David. *Dialogues Concerning Natural Religion and Other Writings*. Edited by Dorothy Coleman. Cambridge: Cambridge University Press, 2007.
Hunt, John Dixon. *The Figure in the Landscape*. 2nd ed. Baltimore, MD: The Johns Hopkins University Press, 1989.
Huxley, Julian. *Ants*. London: J. Cape and R. Ballou, 1930.
Idel, Moshe. "*Deus sive Natura*—The Metamorphosis of a Dictum from Maimonides to Spinoza". In *Maimonides and the Sciences*, edited by Robert S. Cohen and Hillel Levine, 87–110. Dordrecht: Kluwer Academic, 2000.
Isidore of Seville. *The Etymologies of Isidore of Seville*. Translated by Stephen A. Barney et al. with the collaboration of Muriel Hall. Cambridge: Cambridge University Press, 2006.
———. *Traité de la nature (De natura rerum liber)*. French & Latin. Edited and translated by Jacques Fontaine. Paris: Institut d'études augustiniennes, 2002.
Larkin, Philip. *Collected Poems*. Edited with an introduction by Anthony Thwaite. New York: Farrar, Straus, Giroux, 1989.
Lewis, C. S. *The Discarded Image: An Introduction to Medieval and Renaissance Literature*. Cambridge: Cambridge University Press, 1964.
Lindsay, Mark R. *Barth, Israel, and Jesus: Karl Barth's Theology of Israel*. Aldershot, UK: Ashgate, 2007.
Lowth, Robert. *Lectures on the Sacred Poetry of the Hebrews*. 1753. Translated from the Latin by G. Gregory, 1787. 4th ed. London: Thomas Tegg, 1839.
Mews, Constant J. "The World As Text: The Bible and the Book of Nature in Twelfth-Century Theology." In *Scripture and Pluralism: Reading the Bible in the Religiously Plural Worlds of the Middle Ages and Renaissance*, edited by Thomas J. Heffernan and Thomas E. Burman, 95–122. Studies in the History of Christian Traditions 123. Leiden: Brill, 2005.
Milosz, Czeslaw. *A Book of Luminous Things: An International Anthology of Poetry*. New York: Harcourt Brace, 1996.
———. *The Separate Notebooks*. Translated by Robert Hass, Robert Pinsky with Renata Gorcznski. New York: Ecco, 1984.
Murphy, Francesca Aran. *Christ the Form of Beauty: A Study in Theology and Literature*. Edinburgh: T. & T. Clark, 1995.
Newman, John Henry. "On Consulting the Faithful in Matters of Doctrine." *The Rambler: Catholic Journal and Review*, New Series, I (July, 1859) 198–230.
Paley, William. *Natural Theology: Or, Evidences of the Existence and Attributes of the Deity. Collected from the Appearances of Nature*. 4th ed. London: Wilks & Taylor, 1803.

Plantinga, Alvin, and Nicholas Wolterstroff. *Faith and Rationality: Reason and Belief in God.* Notre Dame, IN: University of Notre Dame Press, 1984.
Plato. *The Collected Dialogues, including the Letters.* Edited by Edith Hamilton and Huntington Carins. Princeton: Princeton University Press, 1961.
Raven, Charles. *Experience and Interpretation: The Gifford Lectures 1952.* Cambridge: Cambridge University Press, 1953.
Reznikoff, Charles. *The Poems of Charles Reznikoff. 1918-1975.* Edited by Seamus Cooney. Jaffrey, NH: David R. Godine, 2005.
Seneca, Lucius Annaeus. *Moral Epistles.* Translated by Richard M. Gummere. The Loeb Classical Library 1. Cambridge: Harvard University Press, 1917
Sertillanges, A.-D. *La Philosophie de S. Thomas d'Aquin.* Paris: Aubier, 1940.
Spinoza, Benedict de. *Spinoza's Ethics and "De Intellectus Emendatione."* Translated by A. Boyle. London: J. M. Dent, 1910.
Swinburne, Richard. *The Existence of God.* New York: Oxford University Press, 2004.
Thomas Aquinas. *Scriptum Super Libros Sententiarum Magistri Petri Lombardi Episcopi Parisiensis.* Vol. 1. Edited by R. P. Mandonnet. Paris: P. Letheilleux, 1929.
Thunberg, Lars. *Microcosm and Mediator: The Theological Anthropology of Maximus the Confessor.* 2nd ed. Chicago: Open Court, 1995.
Weinberg, Steven. "Without God." *The New York Review of Books* 55:14 (2008) 73–76.
Witherbee, Winthrop. *The Cosmographia of Bernardus Silvestris.* New York: Columbia University Press, 1973.
Wonham, Jonathan. "The Ant Analogy." No pages. Online: www.http://qarrtsiluni.com/category/insecta/
Wright, James. *Above the River: The Complete Poems.* Middletown, CT: Wesleyan University Press, 1990.

www.ingramcontent.com/pod-product-compliance
Lightning Source LLC
Chambersburg PA
CBHW030857170426
43193CB00009BA/639